Praise for *Crazy Good Sex*

In this culture, it's difficult for men to maintain a healthy perspective of human sexuality and sex in marriage. *Crazy Good Sex* is just what the doctor ordered ... Dr. Les Parrott, of course. This book is going to give you a LOT of new understanding.

> DR. DENNIS RAINEY
> President of FamilyLife

I love this book! Les Parrott has a gift for making important information easy to understand. And that's abundantly clear in *Crazy Good Sex*. Every man needs this valuable information! I urge you to read this book. It is sure to positively change your sex life!

> GARY SMALLEY
> Author of *The Language of Sex*

Les Parrott has a great gift of getting right to the point. Each of his books seem to do just that. Now, *Crazy Good Sex* clarifies and demystifies the issues of male sexuality. Every man (and his wife) will benefit from this straightforward, no holds barred, discussion of the subject that captivates much of our thinking. He even does it with great humor!

> LOUIS McBURNEY, MD
> Founder of Marble Retreat

Every guy should read this book! I promise you that your sex life will never be the same. Dr. Parrott is immensely practical and thoroughly grounded. Not only will you be glad you read it, but so will your wife!

> DR. KEVIN LEMAN
> Author of *Sheet Music*

Have you ever wanted to grab a cup of coffee, sit on the back porch with a wise mentor and ask him questions about sex you always wanted answers to … real answers? Dr. Les Parrott gives you that opportunity with his book *Crazy Good Sex*. Les tackles the topics most "experts" dodge — and he does it with candor, respect, and biblical insight.

DR. GARY ROSBERG
Coauthor of *The 5 Sex Needs of Men and Women*

Read this no-nonsense book by Les Parrott and you're sure to improve your sex life. Every man needs this book!

STEPHEN ARTERBURN
Author of *Everyman's Battle*

Men are in a crazy sexual war that can rip the heart out of a marriage and deaden one's hope in the power of the gospel to change our inclinations. Les Parrott offers a wise and compelling path to honestly face our struggles and to taste the sensual, passionate joy of our sexuality that honors love and rejoices in pleasure. This is a book that will transform you.

DAN B. ALLENDER PhD
Author of *The Wounded Heart*

Every man (and woman) should read *Crazy Good Sex*! This book will transform your sex life. Dr. Parrott is grounded, practical, and accessible. He tackles the issues others are afraid to talk about and he does so with clarity and wisdom. Do yourself a favor and read this book today.

DR. TIM CLINTON
President of the American Association of Christian Counselors

There are two kinds of men. Men who struggle with sex. And men who are dead. The former will find this book incredibly helpful.

MARK DRISCOLL
Founding Pastor of Mars Hill Church,
President of the Acts 29 Church Planting Network

When it comes to men and sex, there are a lot of lies masquerading as foregone conclusions. They've been hammered into us by the uninformed and misguided voices that surrounded us in the locker rooms, boardrooms, and bar rooms of our life. Left unchallenged, these lies are guaranteed to steal the fun and ruin the excitement between a man and his wife. Les Parrott punches the lights out of six of the biggest myths holding men's marriages hostage. The truth, indeed, will set you free. You're going to really appreciate this book.

> Dr. Tim Kimmel
> President of Family Matters
> Author of *Raising Kids for True Greatness*

Finally, a book that offers men the unblushing truth about the oft-repeated and now exposed real-life, nitty-gritty, secret myths that so many Christian men have thought or been taught about sex. Dr. Les Parrott's biblically grounded, evidence-based, and practical answers to these myths are sure to be a boon to increasing your sexual health.

> Walt Larimore, MD
> Coauthor of *His Brain, Her Brain*

Crazy Good Sex is clever and candid. Speaking man to man, Dr. Les Parrott offers information and advice for any man wanting to understand sex and sexuality as the Designer intended. You will enjoy the myth-busting honesty of this gifted communicator and counselor.

> Dr. Ed Young
> Pastor, Second Baptist Church, Houston, Texas

This book should be in the hands of every man who desires to be godly while also being the superb sexual creature God designed him to be. Never preachy, always empathetic, and continually providing practical guidance, Les Parrott has written with courage, transparency, and power. It will be surprising if men get a chance to buy it for themselves because their wives will beat them to it. I heartily recommend it not just for men, but for teenagers growing into manhood.

> Joe Beam
> Founder and President, Family Dynamics Institute

Les Parrott does it again! A straight-in-your face read with significant and practical implications. Read this book and discover God's design for your sex life!

ERIK REES
Saddleback Church Pastor of Life Mission
Author of *Only You Can Be You*

God calls us to not conform to the ways of this world, and Les Parrott has done a remarkable job of showing us the sexual myths that men should not conform to. With great courage, honesty, and sensitivity, he points us to the real truth. All men should read this book, and dare I say their wives will love them for doing so.

MARK R. LAASER, PhD
Founder and President, Faithful and True Ministries, Inc.

Having counseled thousands of couples through sexual struggles, we can verify that Les has tapped into the key issues for men. In his inviting, innovative, refreshing, and always current style, Les gives men the words they need to move from their stuck misconceptions to true freedom as they embrace the naked truth!

DR. CLIFF and JOYCE PENNER
Authors of *The Gift of Sex*

A book like this is long overdue and much needed. Les Parrott expertly tackles many of the most critical sexual issues facing men (and women) today. I highly recommend *Crazy Good Sex*. Every man could benefit from reading this book.

GARY THOMAS
Author of *Sacred Marriage*

Les Parrott answers the questions men are asking. As a wife of many years, I laughed, learned, and eagerly read the Notes to the Curious Woman. After reading this excellent book, both husbands and wives will thank God that the myths men have about sex are being put to bed!

LINDA DILLOW
Coauthor of *Intimate Issues* and *Intimacy Ignited*

Books by Les Parrott

3 Seconds*
25 Ways to Win with People (coauthored with John Maxwell)
The Control Freak
Helping Your Struggling Teenager
High Maintenance Relationships
The Life You Want Your Kids to Live
Love the Life You Live (coauthored with Neil Clark Warren)
Once Upon a Family
Seven Secrets of a Healthy Dating Relationship
Shoulda, Coulda, Woulda*

Resources by Les and Leslie Parrott

Books

51 Creative Ideas for Marriage Mentors
Becoming Soul Mates
The Complete Guide to Marriage Mentoring
Getting Ready for the Wedding
I Love You More (and workbooks)
L.O.V.E. (and workbooks)
Just the Two of Us
Love Is . . .
The Love List
Love Talk (and workbooks)*
Meditations on Proverbs for Couples
The Parent You Want to Be*
Pillow Talk
Questions Couples Ask
Real Relationships (and workbook)*
Saving Your Marriage Before It Starts (and workbooks)*
Saving Your Second Marriage Before It Starts (and workbooks)*
Trading Places (and workbooks)*
Your Time-Starved Marriage (and workbooks)*

Video Curriculum—ZondervanGroupware®

Complete Resource Kit for Marriage Mentoring
I Love You More
Love Talk
Saving Your Marriage Before It Starts

*Audio version available

crazy good sex

putting to bed the myths
men have about sex

Dr. Les Parrott

ZONDERVAN.com/
AUTHORTRACKER
follow your favorite authors

We want to hear from you. Please send your comments about this book to us in care of zreview@zondervan.com. Thank you.

ZONDERVAN

Crazy Good Sex
Copyright © 2009 by The Foundation for Healthy Relationships

This title is also available as a Zondervan ebook. Visit www.zondervan.com/ebooks.

This title is also available in a Zondervan audio edition. Visit www.zondervan.fm.

Requests for information should be addressed to:
Zondervan, *Grand Rapids, Michigan* 49530
This edition: ISBN 978-0-310-33487-3 (softcover)

Library of Congress Cataloging-in-Publication Data

Parrott, Les.
     Crazy good sex : putting to bed the myths men have about sex / Les Parrott.
        p. cm.
     Includes bibliographical references (p.196).
     ISBN 978-0-310-27356-1 (hardcover)
     1. Sex—Religious aspects—Christianity. I. Title.
BT708.P37 2009
261.8'357—dc22   2008045545

Published in association with Yates & Yates, www.yates2.com.

Some names have been changed to protect the privacy of individuals.

Cover design: Michelle Lenger
Cover photography: ©Chad Johnston / Masterfile
Interior design: Beth Shagene

Printed in the United States of America

To my two little boys, John and Jackson,
who may someday read this book
in the appropriate season of their lives.
I pray you will become men who refuse
to separate sex from the sacred.

Contents

PART TWO
Six Big Sex Myths

Acknowledgments

I never dreamed about writing a book like this. It wasn't part of my professional plan. The focus of most of my writing is on skills for improving relationships – especially marriage. My wife, Leslie, and I have written several books together on the subject. And, until now, we've always left the intimidating topic of "sexuality" to others.

But in the past few years it became more obvious than ever to me that a book like this was begging to be written. And a meeting with a group of men in Seattle some months ago served as a catalyst for me to put the proverbial pen to paper. I'm deeply grateful to Dudley Delffs, Scott Bolinder, and Sealy Yates. Without them, I would have never written the book you're now holding.

I've got to confess I've never had more people – both men and women – review a manuscript than I have this one. When dealing with such a personal and important topic, I wanted to be sure I had as many wise minds in the process as possible. I owe deep appreciation to all of them.

I'm especially grateful to Dr. Cliff and Joyce Penner, two of the most studied Christian sexual therapists I know. They reviewed this manuscript in-depth and made numerous helpful suggestions based on their decades of pioneering clinical work with countless clients. The endnotes to this book don't do justice to their added value.

Some of the people who were also particularly generous with their time include Norm and Bobbe Evans, Clinton McLemore, Linda Dillow, Steve Moore, Doug Engberg, Shane Fookes, Rob McKenna, Kevin Lunn, Monty Lobb, Mark Brown, Jeff Kemp, Michael Roe, Matt Whitehead, Larry Roberts, Gary Gonzales, Michael Smalley, Ben Young, Matt Wimmer, Tim Gaydos, Phil Herzog, James Smith, Michael Boerner, Kevin and Robin Small, Jeff Judy, Michael Ranville, Ken Coleman, Jeana Ledbetter, Phil Herzog, Tom Dean, George Toles, and Sandy VanderZicht. I also owe a special debt to my long-time editor, and newly married, Becky Philpott.

I'm so grateful to "the team" that makes what I do easier: Johanna Cabrera, Sarah Schleiger, Bill Dallas, and Janice Lundquist. I can't say thanks enough.

And finally, to my wife Leslie. You are more than I could ever ask or dream.

Love is the answer, but while you are waiting for the answer, sex raises some pretty good questions.
Woody Allen

How to Get the Most
from This Book

No human longing is more powerful, more difficult to rein in, than sex. It has enough combustive force to incinerate wedding vows, family commitments, career goals, religious devotion, and anything else in its path. This book is designed to help any man who wants to keep the combustive force of sex from wreaking havoc in his life—while not diminishing the fire of his sexual fulfillment.

How will this book help? By breaking apart six common myths that, in all likelihood, are doing far too much damage to your sex life. You may not believe these myths outright, but you may find yourself influenced by them without even realizing it. After all, it's sex that most often confounds understanding. It's sex that raises the most questions and leads us to believe crazy misnomers and myths. And it's high time we put these destructive fallacies to bed.

But I want you to know I've written this book to be encouraging—not condemning. You won't find a guilt trip in these pages. I don't want you to feel ashamed or embarrassed. I want you to feel informed and supported in being the man you want to be. I hope you'll draw closer to God's grace and truth as you read.

Consider a Small Group

If you are in a small group with other men, you probably already recognize the value of reading this book and then talking about it together. Few topics make for more lively and engaging discussion in a group of men than the issues in this book. For this reason, I've provided a few questions for reflection at the end of each chapter.

By the way, if you're not in a small group with other men and you'd like to be, you may want to consider this book as a tool for starting one. Simply invite a few guys to meet with you for just a few weeks to discuss the chapters in this book.

Of course, you don't have to be in a small group to benefit from this message. If you're reading the book on your own, you'll find the questions for reflection at the conclusion of each chapter just as meaningful to ponder.

Crazy Sex on the Internet

It's not what you're thinking. This book has a robust online experience to accompany your reading—and it's completely free. I hope you'll join me and other readers on an exciting journey with *Crazy Good Sex* at my online Journey Log™ — or jLog™ for short. Got to www.Crazy-GoodSex.jLog.com to get started.

The *Crazy Good Sex* jLog™ is designed with you in mind. It will take you through an interactive video experience that allows you to engage more deeply with the book, with other readers, and with me. I think you'll enjoy it. I've placed a reminder at the conclusion of each chapter to help you take advantage of this unique resource.

Ask Me Your Questions

Finally, if you have questions as you're reading this book, I hope you'll let me know. My website is designed to be a two-way street. It contains well over a thousand free video-on-demand pieces that were generated from questions we receive on a daily basis at RealRelationships .com. So please, don't hold back. Shoot your questions my way and you'll eventually receive a video response.

> With every good wish and prayer,
> LES PARROTT, PhD
> Seattle, Washington

A Brief Word
to the Curious Woman

When I finished writing this book, I had a couple dozen guys I respect read and critique it for me. Their feedback was invaluable. But I soon realized that several of these men also included unsolicited feedback that came from their wives. The men would say something like this in an email to me: "By the way, Lisa also read the book and thought that ..." And, of course, my own wife, Leslie, seemed to be pretty curious about what I was writing as well.

It didn't take me long to figure out that there may be more than a few women who pick this book up to peruse it before giving it to their husband as a gift or because their husband is already reading it.

So, let's admit it. You're curious to know what your man is reading about sex. I don't blame you. In fact, I think it's a good thing. Of course I've written this book directly to men. That's my audience. But since I know you might be looking in, I'm going to make it easy for you.

In each of the "Six Big Myths" chapters you'll find a little section on a single page that I'm devoting specifically to you — "the curious woman." It's nothing major. Just a related thought I have for you as a woman who has a husband reading this material.

So don't feel guilty. Don't fear that you're eavesdropping. I'm inviting you to listen in.

Crazy Sex
or Stupid Sex?

PART ONE

CHAPTER 1

Kinky and Corny: The Honest Reason I Wrote This Book

Anyone who seeks to destroy the passions instead of controlling them is trying to play the angel.

Voltaire

For over a decade, I've been giving a lecture on human sexuality in the largest classroom auditorium we have on the Christian college campus where I teach. And every year, with two hundred students present, I start the class with this sentiment: "When it comes to sex, there's a lot of crazy thinking." I'll pause long enough for students to wonder where I'm going before giving an example.

"How many of you had corn flakes this morning?"

Dozens of hands shoot up around the room.

"And did any of you consider the fact that you were eating a food that was developed in an effort to curb your impulses to masturbate?"

Looks of puzzlement give way to giggles, followed by a crescendo of side-comments that fill the room for an inordinate amount of time. I walk the lecture stage until the buzzing dies down and my bemused students give me their attention in exchange for an explanation.

"It's true," I tell them as a large box of corn flakes slowly emerges on the giant PowerPoint screen behind me. "They were developed by a physician in Battle Creek, Michigan, who wrote that neither the plague, nor war, nor smallpox, nor similar diseases, have produced results so disastrous to humanity as the unhealthy habit of masturbation. He felt that this 'self-abuse' destroyed not only moral well-being, but physical and mental health as well."

The solution? Corn flakes, naturally.

His name was Dr. John Harvey Kellogg. He created a mixture of oatmeal and corn meal, baked it into biscuits, then ground the biscuits to bits and prescribed them to diminish the human sex drive — even among married men. Why? He believed sexual activity caused cancer, urinary disease, impotence, epilepsy, and insanity. He also claimed that masturbation was a pri-

> *The sexual part of us is a simple yet complex aspect of our being.*
> *It is predictable, yet changeable, diverse, unknowable, mysterious, and forever beyond our full understanding. If this sounds confusing and contradictory — it is.*
>
> **Cliff and Joyce Penner**

mary cause of acne, heart disease, atrophy of the testicles, sleeplessness, loss of vitality, and vision impairment.

Pretty good reasons not to skip breakfast, don't you think?

Charles William Post did. He was one of Kellogg's patients who quickly spotted the commercial possibilities and started his own cereal business. The corn flake race was on. First, there were Post Toasties, then Korn-Kinks (I'm not making this up!). No fewer than forty-two varieties appeared on the market in the late nineteenth century. But Kellogg's Corn Flakes became king.

By the way, Dr. Kellogg's doom-and-gloom views on sexuality couldn't help but impact his honeymoon. That's when

> *Sexuality throbs within us as movement toward relationship, intimacy, companionship.*
>
> **Lewis Smedes**

he began writing the eventual 644-page *Plain Facts for Old and Young*, a warning on the evils of sex. He and his wife of more than forty years had separate bedrooms all their lives, not surprisingly.[1]

What *is* surprising is that some of Dr. Kellogg's views on sex are still held today — even though corn flakes survived because of their taste rather than their "health benefits." In our contemporary culture, we *still* have lots of crazy thinking surrounding sex. The difference is that it's focused more on self-indulgence than on self-control.

And this crazy thinking (not to mention behavior) is exactly why I wrote this book.

Crazy Good or Crazy Bad?

As a psychologist who, with my wife, Leslie, has written a number of marriage books, given hundreds of marriage seminars around North America, conducted university research studies on human sexuality, and counseled countless couples about their most intimate of interactions, I've seen my share of not-so-sane thinking about sex — especially among seemingly smart men.

I want you to know that because of what I have encountered, I feel compelled, if not called, to write about sex and the modern man at a very personal level. You won't find this book to be a clinical treatise or a biological exposition diagramming where you can find your wife's clitoris. Nope. This is a guidebook designed to dispel the crazy thinking and behavior that surrounds sex.

This book is designed to shed light on what distinguishes "crazy good sex" from "crazy bad sex" — or "normal and healthy sex" from "sick and dysfunctional sex." I want to help you draw a dividing line between what's common and what's kinky, what's truth and what's fiction. After all, that line has grown increasingly fuzzy in recent years. It's time we trade in folklore for facts and dispel the myths and illusions men have about sex.

Other Men Don't, But You Do

I'll tell you straight-out that I am making some assumptions about you. To begin with, I assume you are monogamous. I assume you're living a relatively balanced life—that you're not living on the sexual fringe. I assume you are a rational man with good, solid values. And it's precisely because you *care* about being a good man that you experience sexual struggles. Other men don't care to try, but you do.

If you are single, I assume you will eventually be married, since nine out of ten people marry at some point in their lives.[2] So in the portions of this book where I address sex in marriage, I don't want you to feel excluded. I want you to digest the information as you prepare for your married life. I have you in mind, too, even if I'm not going out of my way to clumsily qualify each point for the single male.

> For as he thinks in his heart, so is he.
>
> **Proverbs 23:7 NKJV**

If you're married, I assume you want everything God intended you to enjoy in your marriage—including crazy good sex. But I also assume you sometimes wish sex with your wife was more passionate, more creative, more often—in short, more unbridled. I also assume you have a powerful sex drive and that you want to focus your passionate urges on your wife in a healthy way, but your libido can come dangerously close to getting you into trouble at times. In the words of Jesus to Peter at Gethsemane: "The spirit is willing, but the body is weak" (Matthew 26:41). I assume you want to protect your marriage against mismanaged sexual urges — the kind that lead to addictions and affairs. And I assume you also face countless temptations — the Internet, men's magazines, adult channels in your hotel room, "gentlemen's clubs," and attractive coworkers. In fact, I assume you face these kinds of temptations daily. What's more, I assume that some of you, my readers — normal, rational, and good — have already done some crazy things you're not proud of. That's where the redeeming power of God's grace is experienced most profoundly (see John 1:16).

I am also making an important assumption about your personal faith. I assume you have a relationship with God, that you sincerely try to follow Jesus, and that you want to live a life grounded in biblical principles and Christian qualities — free from "sexual immorality" (see 1 Corinthians 6:18). And I assume your religion has shaped your sexuality, for good and for bad.

Most of all, I assume you want guilt-free, crazy good sex with your wife — and I assume that sometimes some of your beliefs and feelings get in the way.

Debunking the Crazy Myths
Men Have about Sex

I'll let you in on a little secret. When I started writing this book, I thought I'd title it "Crazy Sex." Every author is looking for a way to cut through the clutter of the hundreds of other books out there and I thought that might do the trick. Well, after a few of my most respected friends reviewed the manuscript, I realized that not every man would feel at ease sitting in a coffee shop reading a book with those words on the cover. But when that was the working title of the book, most men asked me flat-out: "Are you talking about crazy good sex or crazy bad sex?" The answer is both.

Men struggle with sex. Especially good men. And many of our sexual struggles stem from our crazy thinking about sex. Why? Because our beliefs determine our behavior. If we *believe* crazy things about sex, we *do* crazy things in our sex lives.

> *Anybody who believes that the way to a man's heart is through his stomach flunked geography.*
>
> **Robert Byrne**

In this context, I'm talking about "crazy bad sex." And because sex is so powerful, crazy thinking can cause even smart men to do stupid things. But once we straighten out some of our misguided thinking about sex, our sex life inevitably improves.

Trading in falsehoods for facts can't help but improve the odds of your sexual fulfillment. It can't help but cause you to increase the probability of enjoying "crazy good sex" in your marriage.

That's why my main objective in this book is to dispel some of the most damaging myths—the crazy thinking—men have about sex. I've surveyed men formally and informally for the last several years, and I've found a predictable set of misguided beliefs about sex that has caused too many of us to struggle needlessly. It's these myths I intend to expose and dispel.

Specifically, I'm going to expose the myths we hold about our "uncontrollable" sex drive and how to please a woman between the sheets.

The man and his wife were both naked, and they felt no shame.

Genesis 2:25

And yes, I'm going to show you what research has to say about the false belief so many men have about the size of their penis. By the way, the crazy thinking on this one underwrites an entire industry for gullible men—pills, pumps, surgery, you name it. It deserves to be dispelled.

I'm also going to surprise you with evidence indicating that what you believe about your wife's sex drive, in relation to your own, may not be quite on target. Correcting just this single false belief may be enough to improve your sex life twofold.

I'm going to reveal the lie men believe about limiting themselves to sex with the same woman, year after year. You'll soon see how married sex is the best sex — and how it should get better and better over time.

I'll also expose "the porn norm." I'll show you how pornography can harm you and your masculinity (not to mention your marriage) in ways you never considered.

And before we're done, I'm going to shatter a belief you may have that is preventing you from having the best sex of your life. Every sex therapist seems to know this secret, but the word just isn't getting out.

In short, I intend to right the wrong thinking men have held about sex for far too long.

For Reflection

1. What's the craziest bit of misinformation, or the silliest myth, you've ever heard about sex?

2. Of the assumptions made about you as a reader of this book, are there any that are not true? If so, which ones and how?

3. What drew you to this particular book and what is one thing you would like it to do to improve your sex life?

 Check this out! You'll find a special online video feature specifically designed to augment what you have just read in this chapter, along with a message from Dr. Parrott. Go to **CrazyGoodSex.jLog.com/Ch1** to find the jLog for this chapter.

CHAPTER 2

What Hugh Hefner Never Figured Out

Women were the major beneficiary of the sexual revolution. It permitted them to be natural sexual beings, as men are.

Hugh Hefner

Television host Bill Maher, known for his political commentary, was recently discussing some "rules for relationships." With three women guests on the panel, he said, "Don't [gripe] about porn."

When they asked what he meant, he responded, "Unless you [women] are willing to give us sex whenever we want, you don't have the right to gripe if we use pornography."[1]

After hearing his explanation, all three women readily agreed that the rule made sense. Surprised? Most aren't. Maher's rule and the response from these women simply demonstrate the prevalent view our contemporary society holds about men and sex. That is, the purpose of sex for men is primarily personal pleasure and we won't be denied it.

Of course this attitude didn't start with Bill Maher. He was simply drinking the Kool-Aid of an unknown copywriter in Chicago who stirred up the belief decades earlier when he started a maga-

play·boy: *a man who pursues a life of pleasure without responsibility or attachments.*

zine called *Playboy*. Pasted up on a card table in his apartment, the first issue featured a centerfold of Marilyn Monroe reclining nude on a carpet of red satin. Of course, that man was Hugh Hefner. And he was not only selling a magazine—he was selling sex. More specifically, he was selling a new sexual ethic. He was doing nothing less than starting a revolution by asking 1950s America to trade in its "sexual repression" for what he called "a liberated lifestyle."

In the postwar era of the 1950s, skin magazines and smut films were only available to those who knew where to find them, typically at back-alley newsstands or seedy adult theaters. Hefner wanted to change all that. But how do you take such an upheaval of hedonistic values main- stream? The key for Hefner was to create an upscale image for *Playboy* and carefully edge it toward the middle. As one commentator says, "he combined *Esquire*'s literary sophistication with the sort of artful nudes one could find in camera magazines like *Popular Photography*."[2]

Unlike other men's magazines of the day, *Playboy* didn't run crime stories or articles about fishing. From the start, it emphasized being stylish, in-the-know, and cool. "We enjoy mixing up cocktails," he wrote in the first issue, "putting a little mood music on the phonograph, and inviting in a female acquaintance for a quiet discussion on Picasso, Nietzsche, jazz, sex."

Nothing too overt, just subtle and sophisticated.

Hip Like Hef

In 1959, Hefner began a syndicated television program to show men what the bachelor pad lifestyle could be like. Every week, a party was in progress, and Hefner, wearing a tux, invited viewers inside to meet his pals and mingle with "the girls."

Innocent and harmless, right? That was his idea. So was he really on a crusade to rewrite the system of sexual ethics for our day? Absolutely. He made that abundantly clear. His strategy was to remove the shame from self-centered sex by linking the pornographic lifestyle to cultural respect, big money, and political power. His goal was to free men from self-restraint and eliminate what he called "the evils of sexual inhibition."

In 1962, with one of the fastest-selling magazines in publishing history, Hefner wrote "The Playboy Philosophy," a manifesto attempting to explain how Puritanism had led our nation into sexual repression that demanded a transformation. But Hefner stopped composing his credo when he saw the cultural transformation he was demanding well on its way—much faster than he thought. By the mid–1970s, his empire included not only his magazine, but also movie production, casinos, resorts, and an international chain of private clubs where waitresses dressed as "bunnies," complete with ears and tail. The rabbit head *Playboy* logo appeared on countless mainstream products—even air fresheners, hanging from the rearview mirrors in cars of men who were "hip" like Hef.

But during the 1980s, cracks appeared in *Playboy*'s airbrushed façade that would eventually reveal what was beneath the subtle and sophisticated surface of Hefner's cultural empire. Competing magazines offered men far more graphic pictorial spreads. The publisher of *Penthouse*, Bob Guccione, is proud of his own contribution to the sexual "liberation" of Western civilization: "We were the first to show full-frontal nudity." From Hefner's view, *Penthouse*, not *Playboy*, was now leading the way.

When *Playboy*'s sales began to slide, the cover of *Newsweek* put it plainly: "*Playboy*—The Party's Over."[3] But behind the scenes the party was only beginning for Hefner. His dream of moral and cultural upheaval was becoming a powerful reality—and the declining sales of his soft porn magazine were an indicator. Why? Because the "liberated" man of Hefner's world wanted more than scantily clad, airbrushed blondes. Turned out, he didn't want to leave anything to the imagination.

Going Full Frontal

Profits from Hefner's magazine started sinking, but thanks to making porn the norm, he's still rich. Why? Because *Playboy* is heavily invested in X-rated videos. Playboy Enterprises became the first explicitly pornographic business to go public, with shares traded in the stock market. As you probably know, pornography is now a major American industry worth billions annually. But did you know it is worth more than major league football, baseball, and basketball combined? As Matthew Scully commented in the *Wall Street Journal*:

> It was Mr. Hefner who put the real money in porn, a business hard to go poor in under any circumstances (except for the unfortunates given starring roles) and today a $57 billion-a-year global industry. He brought it into the central stream of culture, so that now even upscale bookstores stock *Penthouse* or similar offerings without a second thought. He gave porn that "classy" feel and its phony creed of "artistic" expression and protected "speech" by which far livelier fare than *Playboy* would soon ease into the popular culture.[4]

While upholding *Playboy*'s image as a "classy" publication, selling itself as "soft" porn, Hefner and his company quickly ventured into the "hard core" sectors of the squalid business of pornography. As Scully remarked, "Playboy Enterprises itself, years ago, dropped the pretense of refinement and delicacy, following the money into hard-core cable. Soft-core, hard-core, these were all along just degrees of exploitation and self-debasement and for the procurers a purely legal and commercial calculation."[5]

The mild porn of Hugh Hefner's 1950s dressed itself up in a smoking jacket and pretended for a while to be sophisticated and cool. But it was always just about the business of pornography. It was always about the hedonistic sexual satisfaction of men and nothing more.

So, should we really be surprised when a few decades later Bill Maher proclaimed that one of the rules for relationships is that women shouldn't gripe about pornography if they aren't giving us sex whenever we want? Should it surprise us that three articulate women agreed on national television to this logic? Should it surprise us that none of them pointed to the obvious fact that displaying sex publicly changes and degrades its nature?

Hugh Hefner thinks of himself as a prophet, even a missionary, who has led America out of sexual repression into a new era of sexual freedom. He never admits that it is all based on a lie — probably because he was too intoxicated on his own hedonistic hysteria to even notice. He never figured out that the sexually liberated society he envisioned, and that we now live in, is built on a warped and distorted attitude toward sex. By the standards of today's "liberated" man, the purpose of sex is personal pleasure — and women, along with pornography or whatever else strikes his fancy — are to be used as a means to achieving it. In Hef's world women are merely sexual playthings for male fantasies. Hefner, in his drive to free us from sexual self-restraint and modesty, has neglected to figure out the true purpose and pleasure of sex.

Of course, that's understandable. He's not looking for it. He's not attempting to live his life by God's standards. Quite the contrary. He even scoffs at the idea of sexual morality. He doesn't care to be honorable and monogamous in his sex life. But you and I do. And that's why, for us, the purpose of sex is paramount.

More Than Skin Deep

It's tough, these days, to remember that a man used to be able to wake up to a world without "Girls Gone Wild" or Sex.com, without stunning women modeling lingerie on primetime TV commercials, without cable or Internet porn for all hours and all ages. If you travel, it's tough to recall when you could check into a hotel without pay-as-you-view porn in your room. But, as distant as it might seem, it wasn't all that long ago when you could actually go about daily life without ever encountering pornographic images. That's why, in this sexually saturated society, I dedicate this chapter to helping us — both you and me — recall the real purpose of sex.

We will never recapture the importance of Playboy *in the 60s and 70s because we changed the world. We live in a* Playboy *world now.*

Hugh Hefner

So what is it? Why did God create sex? Procreation is the obvious answer. God clearly gave us sex to make babies (see Genesis 1:22). But he also had something more in mind. God wants us to take pleasure in sex. If you don't believe me, read the Old Testament book, Song of Songs. It is replete with erotic metaphors and sexual excitement. And consider the fact that, unlike most animals that only have sex during the female's fertile period, God created us to *continually enjoy* sexual intimacies within marriage.[6] In addition, the human species is one of very few in which females experience orgasm, and humans continue to have sex long after their childbearing years have passed. You don't have to be a Bible scholar to get this message:

> The husband should fulfill his marital duty to his wife, and likewise the wife to her husband. The wife's body does not belong to her alone but also to her

husband. In the same way, the husband's body does not belong to him alone but also to his wife. Do not deprive each other.

1 Corinthians 7:3–5

As one of my seminary professors once said after reading this passage aloud in class, "The Bible is clear as it can be — it says if you are married, 'Do it!'" He was making his point emphatically because people outside the church (and some deeply religious people) think of God as the great spoilsport of human sexuality, not its inventor. But truth be told, sex is a gift from on High.

Okay, so God created sex for pleasure. But the purpose of sex goes deeper than pleasure. It holds more meaning than "feeling good." Are you ready for this? Sex is not only designed to make you happy but to make you holy. That's right. Sex is as much spiritual as it is physical. Sex can bring you closer to the one who created it.

The ability to make love frivolously is the chief characteristic which distinguishes human beings from animals.

Heywood Broun

When you think of what sex does for you personally, I would guess that making you "holy" isn't the first thing that comes to mind. But hear me out.

Holy Sex!

If the purpose of sex was limited to procreation and pleasure, it would merely be an animalistic act. But for humans, it's about relationship. That's the key. It's a personal
encounter, not just a biological action. Think about how
we humans have sex, compared to other mammals. We
are the only species that commonly copulate face-to-face,
so that partners look at each other as they mate. Why?
Because human sex is designed to be more than physical.
Sex may engage our body, but it also touches our soul.
Perhaps that's why G. K. Chesterton once said, "Every
man who knocks on the door of a brothel is looking for
God."

When we sever the connection of sex from the sacred,
we neglect our spiritual longings. The French sociologist
Jacques Ellul saw our modern fixation with sex as the
symptom of a breakdown in intimacy. Having detached
the physical act of sex from relationship, we become spiri-
tually bankrupt. And I've worked with enough men in my
counseling office to see firsthand the desperate looks of
loneliness and despair when men have compulsively reduced sex to simple self-gratification. It's inevitable when
we neglect the sacred aspect of the gift of sex.[7]

The very word *sex* comes from a Latin verb that means
to cut off or sever, and, as Philip Yancey writes in *Rumors
of Another World*, "Sexual impulses drive us to unite, to

restore somehow the union that has been severed." He points out that Freud diagnosed the pain deep within humans as a longing for union with a parent; Carl Jung diagnosed the same longing as a desire for union with the opposite sex. Christians see an even deeper longing, a longing for union with the God who created them.[8]

Sex has become one of the most discussed subjects of modern times. The Victorians pretended it did not exist; the moderns pretend that nothing else exists.

Fulton J. Sheen

Now let's be honest. Historically, the church has had a tough time getting this one straight. Against the background of a pagan culture, where temple prostitutes were incorporated into worship, the church set up some serious, if not irrational, taboos. Saint Augustine, who was converted out of that pagan background and tormented by his own sexual past, proclaimed that sex for any purpose other than procreation is a sin. The Protestant Reformation eventually brought about a shift in attitudes toward sex. Luther scorned the church's prohibition against marital sex for the sake of pleasure. Yet, in time, the Victorians brought sexual repression back to England and America, even to the extent of covering the legs of furniture, lest they arouse impure thoughts. Talk about "crazy sex"!

But here we are in a new day. We are not so much at

risk for repressing our sexuality as we are for neglecting its spiritual transcendence. We are at risk of losing its meaning by reducing it to mere instinct, a pleasurable biological act, void of a spiritual connection.

What happens when a man connects his spiritual with his sexual sides? Repression? Frustration? Shame? Not if he's relatively healthy. I love what Yancey says: "When I experience desire, I need not flinch in guilt, as if something unnatural has happened. Rather, I should follow the desire to its source, to learn God's original intent." He's saying that a sexual impulse can and should take us to God's original purpose in creating us as sexual beings. He created us for relationship. And a relationship does not get more personal or more sacred than when it is consummated in making love.

To hear many religious people talk, one would think God created the torso, head, legs and arms, but the devil slapped on the genitals.

Don Schrader

I want to say this straight. Sex is more than physical. It's more than treating another human being like a plaything. It is spiritual. And that's why it is designed to make us holy.

Now, I can already hear your questions: "Are you saying that the more sex I have, the more spiritual I am; are you saying that I'm supposed to be thinking religious thoughts while making love?" Of course not. Don't misread me here. You and I both know that sex is complex. It's influenced by mood, levels of stress, constraints of time, sleep, and so on. Remembering that sex is spiritual as well as biological — that it's about a deep and profound connection that resides between two souls — does not guarantee that we will realize anything more than physical gratification in our sex lives.

Sex doesn't promise a spiritual epiphany. After all, marriage is composed of two people who have bad moods, stressful schedules, and imperfect hygiene. As a man, you live with a wife who needs patience, respect, understanding, kindness, nurturing, acceptance, devotion, forgiveness, and so many other honorable qualities. And you need the same from her. Admit it. For when you do, you've recalibrated your sex life for relationship. And that's where the holiness of sex resides.

Every Man's Dream?

Before we leave this chapter and address the myths head on, I've got to ask you a question: Are you envious of Hugh Hefner? Be honest. Don't answer reflexively with spiritual platitudes. Don't answer with how you think you *should* answer. Just be honest with yourself.

As I've been writing this chapter, I could not help but wonder what it would be like to throw off all sexual morals and inhibitions and live the self-indulgent life of Hugh Hefner, complete with "the girls next door" at my beck and call, attending pajama parties and all the rest. After all, as Hefner says, he's living out "every man's dream."

Needless to say, it's not my dream. But it's certainly a fantasy that can't be ignored. I have to admit it. A part of me *is* envious. What man wouldn't like a bevy of voluptuous women in their twenties as playmates?

But would I trade places with him? Not on your life. Like you, I've chosen a different path, one seemingly less traveled in our contemporary culture. You and I have chosen a higher road. But let's not pretend that the part of us that fantasizes about the "Playboy lifestyle" isn't real. Why? Because when we do, we are only deluding ourselves into believing that we are immune to falling off the high road we've chosen to travel. And as we're about to see, that's one of the biggest myths of all.

> *I find there is nothing but godliness in marriage. To be sure, when I consider marriage, only the flesh seems to be there. Yet my father must have slept with my mother, made love to her, and they were nevertheless godly people. All the patriarchs and prophets did likewise. The longing of a man for a woman is God's creation.*
>
> **Martin Luther, theologian (1531)**

For Reflection

1. What would it do for you personally if tomorrow you woke up in a time before *Playboy*, when sexual images were not so explicit in the mainstream as they are today?

2. What do you think about the idea that sex engages not only our body, but also touches our soul? What does this mean to you and how do you personally relate to it?

3. What, if anything, do you envy about Hugh Hefner's lifestyle? Why have you made choices that are opposed to it?

 Check this out! You'll find a special online video feature specifically designed to augment what you have just read in this chapter, along with a message from Dr. Parrott. Go to **CrazyGoodSex.jLog.com/Ch2** to find the jLog for this chapter.

Six Big Sex Myths

PART TWO

Men Want More Sex Than Women Do

Men don't like to cuddle. We only like it if it leads to ... you know ... lower cuddling.

Ray Barone

The scene opens as the camera zooms in on the Barone house at night, and then into the bedroom where Ray is sitting next to Debra, his wife. She's lying down facing the camera, with her back to Ray, about to fall asleep.

Ray, the sports writer in the long-running sitcom *Everybody Loves Raymond,* reaches over and gently touches her exposed shoulder. Eyes closed, Debra simply says, "No." He withdraws his hand, then gently touches her again.

"No," comes the deadpan response. Again, Ray touches her shoulder, and still without moving or opening her eyes, Debra says, "No."

Then, with his brow wrinkled as if conducting an experiment, Ray reaches his hand over his wife's shoulder without touching her.

"No," comes the response — again with her eyes closed. Then, in response to three quick passes through the air over her shoulder, Debra says "No," "No," "No," each in precise timing with the hand passing over her. The scene ends as Ray reaches his hand far above her and, without touching her, swoops it down over her in what looks like an airplane pass. In a pitch that matches the height of the hand she cannot see, Debra responds, "NoooooOOOO."[1]

Ever felt like Ray Barone in this scene? Most married men readily confess to having their sexual advances toward their wife rebuffed on more than one occasion. In fact, most married men believe that women do not want to have sex as much as we do. Over time the old reliable "Not tonight, I have a headache" has morphed into "I'm too tired tonight," but the message to us is the same. They don't want to have sex when we do. Maybe your wife has even accused you of being "insatiable." And you're amazed at how long she can go without ever initiating sex with you.

You know "that look" women get when they want sex? Me neither.

Steve Martin

So, you are wondering how I can be saying this is a myth? Don't men, generally speaking, want more sex than women do?

Though it may seem that way for a variety of reasons,

we are making a mistake to assume just because it so often *feels* that way, that it is true. The fact is that our sex drives, for both men and women, fall along a continuum that looks like a bell curve, and most wives are right in the middle, wanting to have sex with their husbands just as much as their husbands want to have sex with them. Of course, some women actually have a stronger libido than their husband, but these marriages are in the minority.

So why all the hullabaloo about libido mismatch between men and women? And, more importantly, how can correcting this myth lead to better – and more frequent – sex in your own marriage?

I'll begin with a brief lesson on the female libido. Make no mistake, it is more complicated than ours. But if we accurately understand it, we'll not only see that it's unfair to unequivocally say that women don't want sex as much as we do, but we'll also know how to cultivate it more fully. I'll then give you several practical suggestions for getting your seemingly disparate sex drives into the same gear.

What Women Want

In the film *Annie Hall*, Woody Allen and Diane Keaton are shown split-screen as each talks to an analyst about their sexual relationship. When the analyst asks how often they have sex, he answers, "Hardly ever, maybe three times a week," while she describes it as, "Constantly, three times a week."

How is it that a husband and wife can view the frequency of sex so differently? The answer is found, in great part, in understanding how a woman becomes sexually aroused and motivated. Too often, men assume that the way our libido works is (or should be) the same way hers works. But it's not that simple. In fact, it requires a bit of study. "Every woman is a science," said John Donne. And if you take time to study your wife, you will discover that her libido, though quite different than yours, is more powerful than you think.

> *My wife is a sex object. Everytime I ask for sex, she objects.*
>
> **Les Dawson**

Here are some of the most important points in understanding your wife's libido.

Women Equate Sex with Emotional Assurance

One reason for the perceived distinction in male-female motivations for sex is that we are socialized in different ways about sexuality and marriage. Men tend to see sex as a pleasurable, physical activity. In fact, even if you're feeling stressed or out of sync with your wife, you're unlikely to turn down sex with her. Not so for women. Your wife sees sex as a sign of emotional bonding and confidence with you. She needs to feel sure of your emotional togetherness before she can free up her physical togetherness. And if she doesn't feel close and connected with you, your chances for feeling "close and connected" in bed are miniscule.

These separate meanings that the two genders ascribe to sex can become the source of a great deal of miscommunication

Women need a reason to have sex. Men just need a place.

Billy Crystal

and misunderstanding in marriage. Consider the following comments made by a wife and husband who stepped into my counseling office after three or four years of marriage:

WIFE: He keeps saying he wants to make love, but it doesn't feel like love to me. Sometimes I feel bad that I feel that way, but I just can't help it.

HUSBAND: I don't understand. She says it doesn't feel like love. What does that mean, anyway? What does she think love is? I want to have sex with her because I love her!

In this marriage, as in many others, the husband sees himself as showing his love to his wife by engaging her in sexual activity. The wife, on the other hand, sees sexual activity as something that should evolve out of verbal expressions of affection and love. Like a scene from a Woody Allen movie that cuts too close to home, this couple bickers continually about how frequently they have sex—never knowing that their socialization is contributing to their perceived difference in sexual motivation.

Women Withhold Sex When Feeling Hurt

Let's say your wife spoke harshly to you because you left your dirty socks on the floor. You feel she overreacted. You're perturbed. Maybe even angry. A few minutes pass and she walks into your den wearing nothing but a string of pearls around her neck and high-heeled shoes. Now tell me, are you going to punish her by withholding sex because she hollered at you just minutes earlier about your dirty socks?

Apparently, women need to feel loved to have sex. Men need to have sex to feel loved. How do we ever get started?

Billy Connolly

I don't even need to hear your answer.

But you probably need to hear your wife's answer when the roles are reversed. Why? Because unresolved emotional issues, even little ones, are at the root of some low libidos in women. Resentment, unexpressed anger, and hurt feelings can lead some women to withhold sex. Maybe she's too upset with you to let you touch her. Maybe she's hoping that rejecting you sexually will send a message that she either can't bring herself to say or can't seem to get across no matter how often she says it. Maybe she's simply punishing you. Is it right? Nope. Is it fair? No way. Is it healthy? Of course not. But it's a common occurrence, and it rarely registers with men.

Say, for example, she feels like you take her for granted because you don't help around the house as much as she'd like. She thinks, "If he isn't doing something for me, why should I have sex with him?" You'd probably never dream of depriving yourself of sex in order to punish your wife, but women are wired differently. She can put her libido on hold until she regains the "emotional assurance" that tells her you're on her team.

Women Are More "Hormonal" Than Men

When you're feeling frisky and your wife has a "headache," she may actually have a headache! Chances are, to her, it has nothing to do with your sexual desirability. And if you're hearing, "I'm not in the mood" when you want to hear, "Meet me in the bedroom" whispers from your wife, it may be because her mood is being determined by her hormones. Again, it's likely to have nothing to do with your sexual attractiveness. Biological changes are far more likely to sap her libido than they are to sap yours. When was the last time you weren't "in the mood"? Is your memory failing you on this one? If so, that's because, if you're like most men, you can generally get in the mood at the drop of a hat (or any other article of clothing). You're typically not battling a surge of hormones that cause you to question your body image or your wife's acceptance of you.

I have an idea that the phrase "weaker sex" was coined by some woman to disarm the man she was preparing to overwhelm.

Ogden Nash

And let's be honest, we don't have to deal with "that time of the month," and all the hormonal mood swings that can come with it. Not to mention the physical cramping. When she turns you down because she's "too tired," it's most likely true. Getting some shut-eye can sound a whole lot better than getting some action when your hormones are going berserk. You and I, as men, may think, "Well, you'd drift off to sleep a lot easier if you had a feel-good orgasm first." That's true, for men. But (as we'll see more fully in another chapter) sex for a woman doesn't begin with getting naked. It takes more time and work than that.

We are prone to label her "lack of desire" as an overarching condition that pervades the entire relationship when the truth is that she can be very motivated sexually—when her hormones aren't taking her on an emotional roller-coaster ride. Here's the point: For a woman, hormones may mean she feels like having lots of sex at a particular time, rather than sex all of the time.

And to avoid the questions I'm likely to get on my

website, let me tell you exactly when that "particular time" is. It has to do with a neurochemical called oxytocin, often referred to as the "bonding hormone." It spikes right before ovulation, a time when most women are in the mood. And here's some really good news. According to Daniel G. Amen, MD, a psychiatrist, brain imaging specialist, and author of *Sex on the Brain*, oxytocin also helps dull your wife's memory of your annoying traits (like your dirty socks on the floor).[2] In other words, this is also when she is likely to feel most attracted to you.

A Woman's Sex Drive
Can Be More Easily Distracted

Okay. So you've given your wife "the look." It says, "Let's go!" You're ready to rumble. She gets the message but says, "I'll come to bed right after I fold this laundry" … or "make the kids' lunch for tomorrow" … or "take out the recycling." I know. I understand. You can't imagine doing any of those things yourself if your wife were to give you "the look." You're ready to go. *Now.* So why isn't she? The reason is not that men want sex more than women; it's that men are often able to get aroused and sexually ready more quickly than women. This is critically important to understand. I'm not only talking about foreplay once you are between the sheets. That's a given. I'm talking about initiating sex, being ready to even enter the bedroom with sex on your mind.

Allow me to reiterate: women, unlike men, do not separate sex from the emotional aspects of the relationship. Women want a sense of connection that is experienced for more than an hour before approaching the sexual starting line. But they also don't want anything distracting them from it once their sexual engine is about to be turned on. That's why they take more care than we do to go through their mental checklist. They need to be sure the kids are in bed, the door is locked, the shades are shut, and so on. They don't want any loose ends keeping them from focusing on sex once you get started.

According to brain scan research, women's brains are naturally more active than men's, even during sex. The reason: lower levels of the neurotransmitter dopamine. "Dopamine creates the desire to go after a reward – in this case, an orgasm," explains Anita Clayton, MD, clinical professor of obstetrics and gynecology at the University of Virginia.[3] You're more likely to have more dopamine than your wife and that's why you're more goal-oriented when it comes to sex; therefore, you're less distracted.

It's a fact. Your wife is far more vulnerable to distraction from sex than you are and that can keep her sexual engine from starting when you want it to. But don't discount her sex drive because of it. It's just different than yours. If she has an unfinished task, let her finish it. Better yet, help her finish it. You'll be amazed how her libido picks up steam, and you'll be pleased to see how fully present she is while you're making love. An undistracted woman, given time to rev up her sexual engine, will be far more "into it" than a woman who feels pressured and duty-bound to be ready to go at a moment's notice.

How to Align Your "Mismatched Libidos"

In a perfect world, you and your wife would have flaw-lessly matched libidos all the time—but we both know that's never going to be the case. You can't expect to have her sex drive always match your own. But if you're feel-ing like you're being turned down because she's got a "headache" a little more frequently than you should be, I want to offer some practical ideas. After all, perpetual libido differences can drive a big wedge between a hus-band and wife. So for the sake of your marriage, as well as your sex life, it's essential to keep that to a minimum. The following are proven suggestions for putting your two sex drives in the same gear.

Let Go of the Myth

It's true—you find what you're looking for. If you want evidence to indicate that your wife doesn't want sex as much as you do, you'll find plenty of it. But if you're ready to balance the scales of sexual desire, you've got to get over this common male myth by seeing her in a new light. One of the best ways to do this is by putting an end to snide comments or innuendos that highlight a perceived libido difference. Every time you say something, even under your breath, like, "Well, if we ever had sex ...," you're driving a sexual wedge between you. By the way, this means not only forgoing these comments with her, but also when you're out with the boys. Set your mind on seeing your wife on the same side as you. She wants to have a great sex life as much as you do. If you don't believe me, just ask her.

Discuss Your Sex Drives

When was the last time you talked with your wife about her sex drive? It's not a common conversation for most couples. Yet it's critically important for getting your libidos to line up. When the time is right, when both of you are relatively relaxed and not distracted, ask her when she feels most frisky. Her answer may surprise you. I have a friend who told me he recently discovered that his wife found him the sexiest when he wore a suit. He joked about wearing it to bed. The point is that you need to know as much as you can about her sexual desires. Ask her about the time of day, as well as the time of month, when she is most inclined to want to

> *For women the best aphrodisiacs are words. The G-spot is in the ears. He who looks for it below there is wasting his time.*
>
> **Isabel Allende**

have sex. Ask her what would make it easier or more fun for her.

Make Initiations Easier

One of the things I hear from women who are in couple's counseling for this issue is that they don't like to be the one initiating sex. Some women are simply uncomfortable with saying, "Would you like to make love?" If you're married to a woman like this, you've no doubt attributed her shyness in this area to a lack of libido. That's a mistake. Instead, make it easier for her to initiate sex with you. Find a sign or a signal that will make this almost effortless for her. For example, it may be that there's a candle she could light, or a particular song she could play, or a look she could give that would be her signal that she'd like to have sex. You get the idea. So don't waste time. Talk to her about what could be used to make her initiations easier.

Take Your Time

Let's say that to really enjoy sex you need to be in a particular mood. You need to feel completely safe and understood by your wife – and this need begins long before you can even think about jumping into bed. Oh, and to become sexually aroused you need some warm-up time that might begin with several minutes of gentle caressing interspersed with pillow talk. The lights need to be low, you need to consider what you're wearing, and you need some time to brush your teeth and prepare yourself physically.

Hard to imagine, right? But I'm sure you're getting the point. If you want your wife to be more forthcoming with her sexual desires, you've got to do your part in helping her love your love-making sessions. A little understanding can go a long way in getting you to slow it down a bit and set the stage for passionate sex that makes her feel great.

Reduce Distractions

One of the biggest reasons that this myth of unequal libidos persists is that men rarely give consideration to what is distracting women from sex. After all, most of the time it takes a lot to distract us from the effort! That's why we need to take special care in doing whatever we can to keep distractions for her at a minimum. You probably already know what they are, but if you don't, ask your wife to tell you.

If you have children, they're inevitably going to top the list. So will any emotional or conversational loose ends between you and her or anyone else. She may be distracted by tomorrow's busy schedule, an upcoming dinner party, a doctor's appointment, or an unpaid bill. You name it. So if you want her libido to be raring to go tonight, first find out what might be getting in its way and do what you can to remove it. But—and this is a biggie—please don't try the typical macho move of "fixing" her problem so you can have sex. That is sure to backfire.

Pay attention to what dampens her sexual desires by listening patiently. Bite your tongue if you're about to spout off a quick solution. Make sure she feels understood. That's all. You'll be amazed at how much your "doing nothing" can increase her libido.

Touch Her Feelings before You Touch Her Body

If you want to rev up your wife's sexual motor, you'll need a heartfelt message to turn on her ignition. She's hardwired to become sexually motivated when you romance her, when you whisper those proverbial "sweet nothings" in her ear. It doesn't take much. You don't need to compose a poem. You simply need to let her know how much she means to you. Anything endearing will do. You can say things like, "You mean so much to me," or, "You're the best part of my day." Of course, you have to be genuine when you say these things. If you're just "making a move," forget it. She'll read right through you. Every woman knows the difference between manipulative come-ons and heart-felt expressions.

Help around the House

Okay. I know. I can almost see you cringing on this

one. I'm not intending to put you on a guilt trip if you're already feeling like your wife is haranguing you for not doing your fair share. But let me just state the facts from some recent research, then you

You can't have a healthy libido if you're stressed out.

Liza Tedesco

can determine whether doing a little dusting is worth increasing her libido. A University of Washington study found that men who help with the housework have more active sex lives with their wives than their dishtowel-shunning brethren.[4] That was the bottom line of this scholarly study. Need more incentive? A 2003 University of California study found that women are not only more sexually receptive to men who help clean up at home, they're also actually more physically attracted to them.[5] So you decide.

Tune into Her Hormones

I mentioned oxytocin, the "bonding hormone," earlier. It's what helps your wife get in the mood, and it increases before she ovulates. Well, you don't have to be a biologist to know that this occurs every thirty days. So make note of it. You don't have to tell her if you don't want to, but you can certainly discuss it together. Why not make a date of it? Also, on the topic of hormones, did you realize that as men and women age, our testosterone levels drop? In fact, the decrease in testosterone is slower in women. *So what?* you're asking. Well, this gradual decrease can cause women to desire sex more often than men their own age. That's one of the reasons that women reach their sexual prime much later than men do. And for us middle-aged-and-beyond husbands, that's not a bad thing.

By the way, it should be noted that, in some cases, your wife's lack of desire for sex, especially if it is consistent over long periods of time, may also be the result of a hormonal imbalance. If you and she suspect that this is the case, she should consult with her gynecologist about this possibility, or get expert input from an endocrinologist. Being in balance hormonally — especially having ample testosterone in her body — may kick her sex drive back into gear.

> *The morning is when a man's testosterone peaks in his 24-hour hormone cycle. And Day 13 is when testosterone peaks in a woman's monthly hormone cycle. When these two hormonal peaks intersect, they can set the stage for the best sex all month long.*
>
> **Gabrielle Lichterman**

For Reflection

1. What psychological benefits do men gain by believing that we want sex more than women? Why do we propel this myth?

2. The next time you hear a friend purporting that women don't want sex as much as men, are you likely to correct him? If so, how? If not, why not?

3. From the suggestions given in this chapter, which one do you find most meaningful and why? In other words, which one are you most likely to put into practice first?

 Check this out! You'll find a special online video feature specifically designed to augment what you have just read in this chapter, along with a message from Dr. Parrott. Go to **CrazyGoodSex.jLog.com/Ch3** to find the jLog for Myth 1.

A Note to the Curious Woman about Your Husband's Sex Drive

I'm guessing you may not have seen this myth coming. Most women have bought into it just like the men. You've been fed the idea that your husband's libido is stronger than yours and, if you're like most wives, you've felt guilty for turning down his sexual advances on occasion.

At the same time, you may have also wondered why he didn't pick up on some of the times when you were "in the mood." You may have thought, on occasion, that your sex drive was actually stronger than his.

There are a number of reasons for this, but what matters here is the solution. What can you do to help? Initiate sex with him more often. That's it! You have no idea what this will do for your marriage. Survey after survey shows that most men wish their wives did this — and most women feel sheepish about doing so.

So how can you do this? Well, when you're ready for some passionate play, don't drop subtle hints hoping he'll figure it out. And you don't have to make a big announcement either. In fact, you can just hand him a simple note that says something like "Meet me in the bedroom in ten minutes." Trust me, most of the time that's all it takes for your man to get the message — and show up early!

Sex with the Same Person Gets Boring

Thrills come at the beginning and do not last.
Let the thrill go and you will find you are living in
a world of new thrills.

C. S. Lewis

Four married guys go fishing. After an hour, the following conversation takes place:

First guy: "You have no idea what I had to do to be able to come out fishing this weekend. I had to promise my wife that I will paint every room in our house next weekend!"

Second guy: "That's nothing. I had to promise my wife that I will build her a new deck for the pool."

Third guy: "Man, you both have it easy! I had to promise my wife that I will remodel the kitchen for her."

They continue to fish, when they realize that the fourth guy has not said a word. So they ask him, "You haven't said anything about what you had to do to be able to come fishing this weekend. What's the deal?"

Fourth guy: "I just set my alarm for 5:30 a.m. When it went off, I shut off my alarm, gave the wife a nudge, and said, 'Fishing or sex?' She said, 'Wear sunblock.'"

There's a cultural presumption that couples are having sex all of the time, and people are embarrassed if they are not. The fact is, sex is like golf. More people talk about it than do it.

Phil McGraw

If only because of the sheer number of jokes on the subject, like this one, it's clear that married couples can find it difficult to have an exciting sex life over the decades. Consider another one:

An elderly couple was sitting together, watching their favorite Saturday night TV program.

During one of the commercial breaks, the husband asked his wife:

"Whatever happened to our sexual relations?"

After a long, thoughtful silence, the wife replied: "You know, I don't really know—I don't even think we got a Christmas card from them this year."

We joke about the excitement of sex dimming over time in marriage, and most think it's true. Too many men, in fact, have come to believe that marriage is the place where sex goes to die. After all, without the thrill and excitement of something new—and with the built-in obstacles of jobs, kids, a house, and numerous sports channels—keeping things hot and heavy in bed can seem virtually impossible.

But is it?

In this chapter I want to unabashedly assure you that sex is alive and well, if not heated and steamy, in the marriage bed. I'm going to let the facts speak for themselves. And you'll soon see that contrary to popular opinion, a married couple's sex life provides the greatest sex life possible. Then, I will give you several proven strategies for increasing the sexual intimacy that you share with your wife. After all, you can do more than you think to insure that your married sex life stays steamy. Finally, I devote a portion of this chapter to the "sex-starved" married couple. So if the shared libido of your marriage has flat-lined, I intend to help you resuscitate it.

The Facts about Long-Term Married Sex

The movie *Old School*, starring Will Farrell as Frank "the Tank," captures the erroneous belief that marriage eventually kills your sex life. Vince Vaughn's character mocks one of his recently married buddies for deciding to have sex with only one person for the rest of his life.

But the real joke, for those in the know, is on him. Why? Marriage actually makes sex better. It's a proven fact.

The fantasy of single guys going out on the town and

"getting laid" every night is just that—a fantasy. According to the landmark 1994 "Sex in America" survey published in the *New England Journal of Medicine*, the people having the most sex are monogamous, married couples. Married people have better sex lives than single people.[1] Indeed, married people are far more likely to have sex lives in the first place. The majority of married men reported engaging in sex with their wife two or three times a week or at least several times a month, while fewer than half the single guys were having sex that regularly. Married people are about twice as likely as unmarried people to make love at least two or three times a week.

Sex may be redeemed in our secular age not by denying it and not by indulging it but integrating it into our quest for depth, loyalty, and permanance in interpersonal relationships.

Edward Thornton

And that's not all: Married sex is more fun. In a recent news report about the sex lives of married couples, ABC's John Stossel interviewed Mark and Dawna Nocera, award-winning professional dancers who teach at their studio in Woburn, Massachusetts. After fifteen years of marriage, they say their sex life has never been hotter. They say a great marriage and great sex is very much like a dance. "Somebody who's just starting out dancing doesn't know anything about the experience that you have 20 years later when you really move," said Mark Nocera. "I think sex is very much like that. It takes a lot of rehearsal to make dancing look that easy."[2]

Consider the facts. Forty-eight percent of husbands say sex with their partners is extremely satisfying, compared to just 37 percent of cohabiting men. That's right. Even couples living together but not married do not enjoy sex as much as married couples! Turns out that cohabiting men are four times more likely to cheat, and cohabiting women eight times more likely, than husbands and wives.[3]

The British health magazine *Top Santé* commissioned a National Sex and Relationship Survey in 2002 and found that sex for married women is just as good as it is for men. Among the findings:

After 14 years of marriage, 63 percent of women still fancy their husband "just as much as when they first met him."

Almost two-thirds of all married women said the "best sex they've ever had is within marriage" (64 percent).

Juliette Kellow, former editor of *Top Sante*, commented, "This survey turns on its head the idea that the best sex is when we are footloose, fancy free, and single. The truth is, truly great sex and deep intimacy are most likely to happen within the trusting, committed environment of marriage."

Kellow is right. But this isn't what we hear—or see

depicted in film or on TV. Married couples are the designated losers in our hormone-obsessed culture. The late-night comics, for example, would have you believe that the sex lives of married couples are in danger of dwindling into either mechanical routine or total extinction. And a University of Chicago study found that married couples in the movies are rarely depicted as having a great sex life.[4]

I want to make sure you're getting this message: The people most apt to report that they are very satisfied with their current sex life are not singles who flit from one sexual encounter to another, but married couples who believe sex outside of marriage is wrong.[5] In fact, "traditionalists" rank an astounding 31 percentage points higher in their level of sexual satisfaction than singles who have no objection to sex outside of marriage. The findings contribute to a growing body of research linking sexual satisfaction to marital harmony, fidelity, and permanence.[6]

Researchers have found not only that sex is better in marriage, but also it is best if you have only one sexual partner in a lifetime. "Physical and emotional satisfaction started to decline when people had more than one sexual partner," the researchers stated.[7] A study at the University of South Carolina revealed that students who engaged in premarital sex reported that they were more likely to be involved in extramarital affairs once they were married.[8] After a review of existing research, David Larson, a senior researcher with the National Institutes of Health, summed it up this way: "Couples not involved before marriage and faithful during marriage are more satisfied with their current sex life and also with their marriages compared to those who were involved sexually before marriage."[9]

Admittedly, the ideal of lifelong passion in marriage is a challenge for many as they juggle time constraints, careers, friendships, and family commitments. But once and for all, let's dismiss the false idea that sex with the same person is inevitably boring. The facts tell a different story. Of course, the challenge is real, too. Every married couple needs help in this area on occasion. That's why it's important to pass along a few secrets to keeping married sex steamy.

The Secrets of Hot Monogamy

The late Wilt Chamberlain had great numbers as an NBA star, but the number he will probably be remembered for most is 20,000. That is how many women the never-married Chamberlain claimed in his autobiography to have slept with. What few may remember though, says columnist Clarence Page, is that Chamberlain "went on to write that he would have traded all 20,000 for the one woman he wanted to stay with for keeps."[10]

Pretty telling, don't you think? Even a guy who had a crazy number of sexual encounters longed for the kind of deep passion and intimacy that is only found in the lifelong commitment of marriage. What follows are some proven strategies for stoking the fire of that kind of passion. Of course, I can't promise you that your lovemaking with your wife will be the sexual equivalent of the Cirque de Soleil as a result of these, but I can promise you that these techniques have proven helpful to countless couples who want to keep passion's fire burning between the sheets of their marriage bed.

Change Your Position

"You want me to put what where?" That question from either spouse is enough to stunt the progress of any couple's lovemaking. But if it's been a long time since you've tried a new sexual position, if you've settled into a "standard position" like most married couples do after a few years, it may be time to shake things up a bit.

Perhaps you've even forgotten that there are numerous options available to you. Let's see. There's the Criss-Cross, the Down Dog, the Slow Climb, the Giddy-Up, the Spoon, the Pinwheel, the Mermaid, and the ever-elusive Spider Web. I'm not confident I even know what most of these are, but I do know that if your sex life is putting you to sleep, a new position will wake you both up. You don't need to check out a copy of the Karma Sutra; there are numerous wholesome helps in this area. Kevin Leman covers the basics of various sexual positions in his book, *Sheet Music,* as do Cliff and Joyce Penner in their book, *The Gift of Sex,* and Doug Rosenau's *A Celebration of Sex.*

Here's the point: There's a powerful tendency in an enduring marriage to favor the predictable over the unpredictable. Yet without an element of uncertainty, we reduce our sexual anticipation and excitement.

Now, I need to put forth a major qualifier on sexual positions. When it's a mind-blowing, bed-rattling orgasm you're after, keeping it simple is typically best. Sure, wild, crazy, never-knew-my-body-could-bend-that-way sex might keep your love life exciting, but if the goal of the moment is to break pleasure records, you can't neglect the basics.

Change Your Sex Schedule

"Before we had kids," said Paul, 34, married 6 years, "sex had been great for my wife and me, but afterward it always seemed as if our timing was off." He went on to tell me that he would be raring to go about the time she wanted to collapse into bed at night. Ever since their daughter was born three years ago, their sex life has never been the same. The solution? They began meeting for "lunch." Since neither of them work too far from home, they meet there once a week on their lunch hours. "It's great," Paul confides, "because we're both wide awake and our girl is with grandma. Plus, doing it during the workday seems kind of illicit — it's almost as if I'm having an affair with my wife." They aren't rigid about the schedule. They simply agree at the beginning of each week when they will have "lunch" together, and the anticipation of those rendezvous is exciting to both of them. In other words, sex isn't always relegated to eleven o'clock at night.

Think outside the Bed

Who said your sex life is limited to your mattress? If you want to spice up your lovemaking, find a new location. Just like a new position increases anticipation and excitement on occasion, so does a unique sexual locale. For example, has it been a while since you've enjoyed sudsy sex in your bathtub or shower together? Or how about steaming up the windows of your car after pulling into the garage from a dinner out — even as a precursor to going to your bedroom? You get the idea. And you've had the thoughts. So why not invite your wife to a new space for a literal change of pace?

Don't Keep Track

One of the sex questions I often get from men when I'm talking in a seminar is, "How often does the typical married couple have sex?" Fair enough. I understand the curiosity behind the inquiry. But the answer can cause some couples to simply check sex off their to-do list. There is no prescription, no magic number. For married couples, the question of frequency will be answered uniquely in terms of concern for the needs and desires of both you and your wife. A "national average" is of little help. You may be doing it five times a week, but if the sex is just so-so, what's the point?

My former professor, Lewis Smedes, says in his book *Sex for Christians,* "The moral issue is never 'how much' sex but whether physical sex is being integrated into a pattern of personal dedication. What happens 'between the times' is more important than how many times." In other words, if you're concerned about keeping the sexual fires burning, don't count how many times you're striking the match. Just enjoy the warmth of knowing and meeting each other's sexual needs and desires.

Get Hands-On Help If You Need It

"A couple of years ago, I just stopped functioning the way I used to," confessed Robert, 44, married 10 years. "Basically, there were times when I couldn't get it up. My wife thought I wasn't sexually attracted to her anymore. And I guess there was some truth to that — after so much time together, and children, I wasn't instantly turned on by her the way I used to be."

Robert eventually saw a urologist who told him it was normal for someone his age not to become erect from the mere thought of sex. He also told him that he needed "manual stimulation." Well, that worked. Once Robert's wife understood that's what he needed to get going, that it was a physiological issue, she was happy to help out.

Enliven Your Senses

Certain smells and sounds can have a Pavlovian affect on your libido. Think about what puts you in the mood, and then designate an enhancer that will signal to your brain and body that it's time to get busy. For example, consider playing a sultry jazz CD. How about some enticing and aromatic lotions you can use to massage each other? Candles can also be scented. I had a couple in marriage therapy a while back who were all about the fragrance of lavender on their linens. You get the idea. Think back to the early days of your marriage when you'd do everything you could think of to set the mood by enlivening all your senses — seeing, touching, smelling, tasting, and hearing. Why not bring back a blast from your past?

Trade Spontaneity for Intention

A fellow psychologist and friend of mine who sees many couples for sexual issues, says, "I urge my patients not to be spontaneous about sex. It's overrated and over idealized." What he means is that sexual spontaneity is more fantasy than fact. It may be Hollywood's favorite form of sexual encounter, but it's not the norm for married couples who enjoy a healthy sex life. Why? Because they are intentional about sex. And to think that the best sex is always spontaneous is simply not true. In fact, it's a myth—one I'm devoting an entire chapter to later in this book.

Have a "Sex Talk"

Very often a husband and wife can be married for many years without ever telling each other what they find most exciting in bed. This is partly because many people remain painfully embarrassed about their sexual needs. But it's also because too much is at stake—namely, the emotional bond between husbands and wives. To gamble it on fulfilling a need that might be seen as odd, selfish, or simply beyond the comfort level of their partners is too risky. And after years pass, it often becomes more and more difficult to reveal a "hidden" desire, because it feels like introducing something foreign into the relationship, not to mention that it's like admitting that you've been fibbing about your sexual desires all that time. But I can assure you that this talk is worth the risk, as long as you do so carefully.

First of all, you need to bring up the subject when you are not having sex, and it needs to be a two-way conversation. That is, you need to not only be telling her about some of your desires but also genuinely interested in hers.

Next, don't be shy about telling what you like, what

you don't like (but be gentle here—you want to make things better, not cause hurt feelings), and what you would like to try.

Ask questions about what your wife likes, doesn't like, and what she would like to try. Be open to hearing what your wife has to say. Encourage her to open up by listening well.

If something is brought up that one of you is uncomfortable with, respect that and move on to the next thing. Never try to force your wife to try something she is uncomfortable with, or make her feel guilty about her feelings and preferences.

The best position is no substitute for a healthy relationship.

Kevin Leman

By the way, if talking about your sex life is too embarrassing or uncomfortable for either one of you, write your thoughts and your questions out for each other. Consider emailing each other. This will obviously take longer but it will accomplish the same goal. I've got to tell you that this simple suggestion of talking to your wife about what you both want in your love life at this stage in your marriage is almost always rewarding. I've given this assignment to numerous couples in counseling, and I know it works.

Woo Your Wife

Okay, this little nugget is about as time-tested as they

come. You've heard it before, but it's always a good reminder. You see, in marriage, men don't feel the need to seduce or to build anticipation – that's an effort we think we no longer need to do now that we have officially wooed our partner. We come to believe that if we're in the mood, she should be too. Of course, that's not the case. You must elicit your wife's desire. Too often, we make the mistake of simply monitoring it. We wait. We observe. We look for signs, a glimmer of an indication that she might be in the mood. That's not the way to approach it. You need to cultivate it, not monitor it. You need to woo her.

Because of what I do for a living, every year around Valentine's Day I receive dozens of requests for interviews with the media. They all want an "expert" to talk about how men can make the most of this day. After doing countless call-in shows on the subject, I can tell you that most men hate this holiday. They don't like the pressure. They feel coerced into having to buy something or do something for their wife just because it's on the calendar. They'd rather cultivate romance and passion on their own schedules.

> *Passion, though a bad regulator, is a powerful spring.*
> **Ralph Waldo Emerson**

Well, that's what wooing a woman is all about. So here's what I suggest: Make up your own Valentine's Day. Write her a little note, buy her a little treat, deliver a cup of coffee to her work, let her sleep late, leave her a loving voice message. Do whatever you'd like to do—just be sure you woo her. Seduce her. This builds the anticipation for a great night of sex. Now I realize you can't do this all the time. The point, in fact, is that this kind of wooing is to be special and surprising. But if you're wise you won't wait for Valentine's Day before you begin again to woo your wife. You'll be glad you did.

Buy a Lock for Your Boudoir

Okay, this last suggestion is a quick one. It may seem obvious, but if the potential for a child entering your bedroom is curbing your sex drives, buy a lock. Use the lock. Enjoy. I've seen too many couples never take this simple step to strengthen their love life. If you're one of them, install that lock on the inside of your bedroom door today.

What to Do If You're in a Sex-Starved Marriage

Let me address an issue that has become painful for far too many couples: the marriage where passion seems to have vanished, excitement has disappeared, and sex has become a thing of the past.

Comedian Ray Romano, who has four kids, including twins, says his comedy is inspired by real life. "After kids, everything changes," he told *Newsweek.* "We're having sex about every three months. If I have sex, I know my quarterly estimated taxes must be due. And if it's oral sex, I know it's time to renew my driver's license."[11]

No doubt about it, humor can help us hide the pain. But if you are in a marriage where sex is becoming a thing of the past, it's no laughing matter. In

> *A successful marriage requires falling in love many times, always with the same person.*
>
> **Mignon McLaughlin**

fact, what you're experiencing actually has a nickname: DINS. It stands for dual income, no sex.

Faced with the frantic pace of modern life – which entails juggling dirty diapers, demanding bosses, and gym workouts – the libidos of dual income couples seem to have gotten lost in the shuffle.

The statistical evidence would seem to show everything is fine. Married couples *say* they have sex 68.5 times a year, or slightly more than once a week, according to a recent study by the highly respected National Opinion Research Center (NORC) at the University of Chicago, and the NORC numbers haven't changed much over the past 10 years.[12] At least according to what people tell researchers, DINS are most likely an urban myth. But any efforts to quantify our love lives must be taken with a shaker of salt. The problem, not surprisingly, is that people aren't very candid about how often they have sex.

When pressed, nearly everyone defaults to a respectable "once or twice a week."

It's difficult to say exactly how many of the 113 million married Americans are too exhausted — or too grumpy to have sex, but some psychologists estimate that 15 to 20 percent of couples have sex no more than 10 times a year, which is how the experts define sexless marriage. A *USA Today* article reports that a whopping 40 million married couples have little or no sexual contact with their spouses. And *Time* magazine recently observed, "Sleep is the new sex."[13] It seems that for some couples, even if they aren't sleeping, they'd rather zone out to Letterman or Leno than have sex.

If you fall into this category, you probably don't care about the statistics, and you don't need to be convinced that marital celibacy is real. But you *do* want some help. And some of the most straight-talking advice you will find on the subject comes from Michele Weiner Davis, author of *The Sex-Starved Marriage*. Recently, I heard Michele speak on the subject to a room full of hundreds of couples struggling with this issue, and she told them exactly what she says in her book: Just do it. Don't wait until you're in the mood.

> *Sometimes sex is great; sometimes sex is kind of so-so; sometimes you'd rather have ice cream and watch television.*
>
> **Marty Klein**

Weiner Davis's Nike approach to helping sexless couples is proving successful. Early in their marriage, Chris and Tara had sex nearly every night. But after Tara gave birth to their first child, she lost interest in sex. Their nightly sessions became infrequent events. In addition to raising the kids, both Tara and Chris work outside the home. Tara says she's just exhausted. Chris also shoulders part of the blame. "I haven't always been the most romantic, getting-her-in-the-mood kind of guy," he says. Since applying the straightforward approach of Weiner Davis and simply having sex whether they are in the mood or not, Chris and Tara say they now have sex almost once a week and are getting back on track to enjoying their love life together.

"Have you ever noticed that although you might not have been thinking sexual thoughts or feeling particularly sexy," Weiner Davis asks, "if you push yourself to 'get started,' it feels good, and you find yourself getting into it?"

The verdict is in. Sex with the same person does not have to go AWOL, and it doesn't have to get boring. Far from it! And even if you are currently caught in the clutches of a sexless marriage, you can literally will your way out of it. Of course, it all comes down to making a decision to do so.

For Reflection

1. Why is it that so many people believe sex with the same person is bound to get boring when, in fact, the research shows the opposite is true?

2. If you were counseling another guy who was considering marriage but was afraid of only having sex with one woman the rest of his life, what kind of counsel would you give him? Be specific.

3. On the personal side, how satisfied are you these days with the amount of sex you are having with your wife? If it's not as much as you'd like, what's one practical application from this chapter you can do to improve it?

 Check this out! You'll find a special online video feature specifically designed to augment what you have just read in this chapter, along with a message from Dr. Parrott. Go to CrazyGoodSex.jLog.com/Ch4 to find the jLog for Myth 2.

A Note to the Curious Woman about "Boring Sex"

What can you do to make sure your husband isn't buying into this tired myth? Very simply, you can surprise him. If you've been married for a number of years, you know what he likes almost as well as he does. Don't neglect that. But don't wear it out either.

Your husband would love it if you made a conscious effort to heat up what's happening between the sheets when you two are in bed. I've surveyed enough women to know that many feel it's not their role to take the lead when it comes to making love with their husband. But let me assure you that your husband would love to see you exert more creative sexual energy in the relationship.

Try a new technique. Make a new move and whisper, "Do you like this?" Surprise him with some new lingerie. Surprise him with a new position, or maybe a new location if that's what gets both of you going. And don't be afraid to ask him what would be new and exciting to him. Most men don't want to have to tell you this — so ask. Better yet, share a new idea with him and ask him to match it. You can even do this with a couple of note cards if it makes you embarrassed to talk about it.

By the way, your efforts here don't have to be focused only on what happens in the bedroom. You may want to be sure you're keeping yourself attractive before you even get close to bedtime. This doesn't mean you have to wear high heels while you're relaxing at home. It simply means leaning into what makes you feel most beautiful as a woman and being conscious of his physical attraction to you.

You get the idea. Surprise your husband every so often and he'll never come close to buying into the myth that sex with the same person gets boring.

Porn Is Not Addictive

*Pornography is the attempt to insult sex, to do
dirt on it.*

D. H. Lawrence

Dumpster diving. That's what we called it. When we
weren't being distracted by a pickup game of stick
ball or street hockey, it was an irresistible activity for
prepubescent boys in grade school living in middle-
class homes. Needless to say, this was not done out of
economic necessity. We weren't scavenging for food. We
were looking for "treasures" that had been discarded by
someone who thought they were junk. We were looking
for things that could become valuable assets in our tree-
house "fort." And the college campus where most of our
parents worked provided the perfect dumpsters outside
each residence hall for this activity (unbeknownst to our
parents).

So, on an occasional Saturday morning when we felt
the fort needed a facelift, we would sometimes scrounge

around the big trash bins looking for a good find. It might be a piece of lumber, an old lamp, or a picture frame. You never knew — and that was part of the thrill. But not too far into our dumpster-diving excursions, one of us stumbled onto a college student's discarded *Playboy* magazine. A hush fell upon the dumpster as we looked over each other's shoulders to see, for the first time, the airbrushed bodies of naked women.

> *The difference between pornography and erotica is lighting.*
>
> **Gloria Leonard**

I can't remember the pictures, but I still remember the feelings — excitement, nervousness, curiosity, guilt, pleasure. It was a veritable cornucopia of confusing emotions. And chances are that you had a similar experience. The average age for first exposure to pornography is eleven. And by age fifteen, 80 percent of boys have had multiple exposures to hard-core pornography.[1]

Since porn exposure is so common, the reasoning goes, it must be relatively harmless. After all, many people regularly watch pornography and still lead productive lives with normal relationships. "Everyone agrees that tens of millions of Americans consume porn.... ministers, PTA members, policemen, teachers, soldiers, dentists and Boy Scout leaders," argues California sex therapist Marty Klein. "The overwhelming majority of them don't rape strangers or emotionally abandon their wives."[2]

Okay. So Klein is correct — sort of. Millions of men *do* view pornography and never rape strangers or abandon their wives. And for argument's sake, we'll say that the percentage of men fueled by porn who do go on to rape — or become convicted pedophiles or registered sex offenders or who engage in sexual abuse, voyeurism, exhibitionism, anonymous sex, and so on — are merely a minority of sexual freaks. That still doesn't eliminate the dozens of other harmful effects normal people suffer as a result of pornography.

The truth is that porn is gaining a stranglehold on mainstream American culture because of messages like Klein's and others, who say porn viewing is harmless and socially acceptable. It is not harmless. Ask the number of casual porn viewers who ended up addicted — those guys who moved from "casual viewing" to being an "addict" with a steady diet of pornography that warped their relationships to the core.

Talk to almost any psychotherapist and they will tell you that porn, just like any other addiction, can wreak havoc on a person's life and family. Respected sex expert Patrick Carnes describes pornography addiction as "the athlete's foot of the mind." It never goes away, and it continually asks to be scratched, promising relief. But to scratch is to cause pain and to intensify the itch. It's an endless cycle.

I dedicate this chapter to taking an honest look at

why so many men who start out with just a casual look at porn end up in serious trouble. We'll start with a quick examination of what it means to be addicted to porn and how it literally changes your brain — not to mention your marriage. Then I'll devote serious attention to helping you protect yourself against falling into the silent addiction to porn and share insights into what you can do if you already have.

Is "Porn Addiction" Real?

Is porn addiction real? Few would argue against this question if they'd ever met Vladimir Villisov. In 2006, this Russian man specially designed his own coffin to accommodate his vast collection of pornography. He literally lined his casket with hundreds of pornographic images. "The girls in those magazines have been my companions for years," said Villisov, then 65, "and I want them to accompany me to the next life."[3]

You think Vladimir may have had a bit of an issue with pornography? Most could easily argue that there's a pretty good chance he was "addicted" to it. But what exactly do we mean when we say this? And is this label warranted?

Let's begin with a definition: Pornography use becomes an addiction when the user becomes obsessed with the behavior, spending large amounts of time online, even in the face of personal and professional consequences (e.g., relationship or financial or work-related problems).

From a clinical perspective, pornography addiction would involve at least five of the following:

- Frequent (several times a week) preoccupation with pornography
- Frequent engagement with pornography over a longer period than intended
- Repeated efforts to reduce, control, or stop the behavior
- A great deal of time spent in activities necessary for viewing porn or recovering from its effects
- Engagement in the behavior when expected to fulfill other obligations
- Important social, occupational, or recreational activities given up or reduced because of the behavior
- Continuation of the behavior despite knowledge of having a recurrent social, financial, psychological, or physical problem that is caused or exacerbated by the viewing of porn
- The need to increase the intensity or frequency of the behavior in order to achieve the desired effect
- Restlessness or irritability if unable to engage in the behavior

Pornography is that which exploits and dehumanizes sex, so that human beings are treated as things, and women in particular as sex objects.

Langly Longford

On top of any combination of five from this list would be the recurrent failure to resist impulses to engage in viewing pornography.

While it is not considered a legitimate disease by some, almost every clinical psychologist would agree that if these criteria are met, the person is diagnosable as addicted to pornography.

This Is Your Brain on Porn

Perhaps the most compelling justification for the reality of a porn addiction is found in the neurochemical changes that take place in a man's brain when he's engaging in the behavior.

Author and psychologist Arch Hart, in his book *Redeeming Male Sexuality*, identifies two powerful brain chemicals that combine to produce the compulsive seeking behavior that's stimulated through pornography. One is the satisfying tension relief of endorphins. These morphine-like molecules are released in the reward centers of the brain's hypothalamus to produce intense pleasure and relaxation.

The second chemical is epinephrine, which creates

arousal, alertness, increased energy, excitation, and an aggressive stance ready for risk-taking or conquest. Pornography arouses both these responses, which combine to hold the addictive features of risk-taking, excitement, and the endorphin pleasure explosion.

Couple these powerfully habituating chemicals with the forbidden aspect of lust and it provokes an enticing stimulus-response behavior. Add in some stressful life factors, like financial pressures, that cause masculine self-doubt and the stage is set. The use of pornography becomes an instant fix that momentarily reaffirms male potency and gives a tranquillizing, temporary relief of stress. And that's what sets the stage for addiction.

When an addict looks at porn, testosterone, dopamine, oxytocin, and serotonin are released, creating what Dr. Judith Reisman refers to as an "erototoxin."[4] The chemical change, which causes the person engaging in the act to have a temporary feeling of euphoria, is a scientific fact. "Pornography really does, unlike other addictions, biologically cause direct release of the most perfect addictive substance," says psychiatrist Jeffrey Satinover. "That is, it causes masturbation, which causes release of the naturally occurring opioids. It does what heroin can't do, in effect."

> The Internet is the crack cocaine of sexual addiction.
> **Jennifer Schneider**

Pornography addicts have a more difficult time

recovering from their addiction than drug addicts, since drug users can get the drug out of their system through detox, but pornographic images stay in the brain forever, according to Mary Anne Lyden, co-director of the Sexual Trauma and Psychopathology Program.[5]

Like any other type of addict, porn addicts become dependent on their "drug." It literally changes their brain activity. And sooner or later, they become trapped within their disorder as they slip from casually watching pornography to being an addict with a dependence upon the new chemical makeup of their brain.

Why Men Get Hooked on Porn

Fortunately, not every man who is exposed to pornography becomes a full-blown addict. Many men resist the temptation to pull up porn on their computer. They view the exposure to blatant immorality as inherently distasteful. And there are also men who see the hypocrisy of professing to be Christian while inviting those images into their minds. Some men simply respect their wife's feelings about pornography and resist out of their love and commitment to their marriage. But for far too many men, the easy access to pornography these days is simply too tough to resist.

Bill Maier, a clinical psychologist at Focus on the Family, a Colorado Springs organization devoted to Christian family values, says calls about pornography to the group's counseling center have doubled in the past five years as the Internet has made sexually explicit images more easily accessible.

Online porn's accessibility, anonymity, and affordability (the three A's of cybersex) all play a role in hooking an individual. Seventy percent of American men ages 18 to 34 view Internet pornography at least once a month.[6] And truth be told, millions of men sit comfortably in church pews every Sunday who haven't told anyone about their quiet predilection toward porn.

According to *Christianity Today* writer John W. Kennedy, "the average addict is double-minded. Part of him desires to live a holy life. Another part wants to gaze at porn."[7] He deceives himself into believing it's just temporary, that he can quit whenever he wants. On top of this, there is the "entitlement factor" that accompanies the practice. It's fueled by believing they are overworked and underappreciated.

The entitlement often begins with a perceived lack of sexual fulfillment in their marriage. They feel partially justified, in a sense, for "innocently" clicking on something that leads to explicit porn. A few clicks later, followed by sexual release, sets the stage for repeating this behavior the next time the urge strikes — until eventually it becomes a routine that slowly controls them.

Of course, the more control men give pornography

over their time, energy, and thought-life, the more devastating it becomes. The downward spiral tends to become reinforcing: The guy feels ashamed, inadequate, and stressed out, and he seeks release through pornography and masturbation; then he feels lousy that he's given in again to the obsessive-compulsive behavior, and his shame is reinforced.

The compulsive porn pattern is so rampant these days because of the Internet, of course. It used to be that sexual addiction was the primary domain of those who had survived sex abuse while growing up. But the Internet changed all that.[8] It's not your father's porn," says psychologist David Greenfield of West Hartford, Connecticut, an expert on Internet behaviors. "With little or no effort, as long as you have a computer, you can access some of the most stimulating content on the planet. There's no delay, no person watching. It's designed to very quickly get to a point where you're not in full control." And because of that, more men than ever are getting hooked on porn.

What Porn Does to a Marriage

I sometimes hear a guy say, "I'm no addict, I'm just a casual porn user" — as if it's completely harmless. That's when I'm reminded of what Mike Genung, author of *The Road to Grace*, wrote: "What might your wife say if you approached her and said, 'Honey, this year I'm going to commit adultery just three times. Once this month, again in July and one last time in December. But I won't touch anyone, I'm just going to masturbate to pictures of other naked women. But it's just me and pictures and I won't actually have sex with another person. Okay?'"

I'll leave it to you to imagine how your wife might respond, but I'll tell you flat-out that even "casual" porn use creates casualties in marriage. And I promise you that a full-on addiction is sure to eventually create major upheaval and havoc for a married couple.

Two 1988 studies about the effect of prolonged consumption of pornography found that for both men and women, porn fueled unrealistic expectations about what sex should be and what their partners should be like, and made them less satisfied overall. Those studies appeared in the *Journal of Family Issues* and the *Journal of Applied Social Psychology*—well before the Internet was widely used.

More than twenty-five years ago, Dr. Victor Cline identified the progressive nature of pornography addiction. Once addicted, a person's need for pornography escalates both in frequency and in deviancy. The person then grows desensitized to the material, no longer getting a thrill from what was once exciting. Finally, this escalation and desensitization drives many addicts to act out their fantasies on others.[9]

He estimates that for up to 10 percent of porn users,

relationships suffer — with many husbands spending so much time online that they cease to have sex with their wives. But even if you're not in that unfortunate 10 percent, you're not out of the clear. Using pornography is bound to create a breach of trust in your marriage. Spouses often view porn as a betrayal or even as adultery. The typical reaction when a woman discovers her husband's habit is shock. Then she feels like she's not good enough. Otherwise, why would he be looking at other naked women?

"I compare it to your house burning down," said Laurie Hall, who divorced her husband because of his porn addiction and wrote about his twenty-year obsession with pornography in her book *An Affair of the Mind.* "It destroys your sense of personhood when you bring all that you are into a relationship and someone chooses to ignore that," she said. "It eats away at the heart of the family."

Pornography can literally tear couples apart. At the 2003 meeting of the American Academy of Matrimonial Lawyers, two-thirds of the 350 divorce lawyers who attended said the Internet played a significant role in divorces in the past year, with excessive interest in online porn contributing to more than half of such cases. "This is clearly related to the Internet," says Richard Barry, president of the association. "Pornography had an almost nonexistent role in divorce just seven or eight years ago."

If you're thinking pornography couldn't shake the foundation of your marriage, consider the findings of Professors Dolf Zillman of Indiana University and Jennings Bryant of the University of Houston. Their studies revealed that repeated exposure to pornography results in a decreased satisfaction with one's sexual partner, with the partner's sexuality, with the partner's sexual curiosity, a decrease in the valuation of faithfulness, and a major increase in the importance of sex without attachment.

I spoke with Mark Laaser, author of *Healing the Wounds of Sexual Addiction,* and he echoed these findings from a personal perspective. A recovering sex addict himself, Mark says he frequently sought out pornography and engaged in extramarital sex for more than 20 years, starting in college and continuing through a career as pastor and counselor. He now runs workshops and consults with church congregations on the issue. "I've seen firsthand the devastation and damage pornography does to marriages and to families," Mark said.

The bottom line is that pornography radically disconnects sex from its intended meaning. God designed human sexuality for us to express an abiding, passionate, and appealing love between a husband and wife, but pornography separates out one aspect of that gift — physical appeal — and focuses exclusively on it. As a result, a husband who views pornography can't help but begin to see his wife in a not-so-flattering light. The studies suggest that looking at sexually explicit materials can make men view women as less attractive by comparison. They see a higher standard of beauty because the bar moves up from what a woman normally looks like to the often digitally enhanced images.

Mark Schwartz, director of the Masters and Johnson clinic in St. Louis, Missouri, says porn not only causes men to objectify women — seeing them as an assemblage of breasts, legs, and buttocks — but also leads to a dependency on visual imagery for arousal. "Men become like computers, unable to be stimulated by the human beings beside them," he says. "The image of a lonely, isolated man masturbating to his computer is the Willy Loman metaphor of our decade."[10]

Protecting Yourself before You Get Hooked

How can you escape from the tentacles of pornographers? After all, what was once only available in seedy adult theaters or shadowy newsstands, today is everywhere. It literally pours into our homes and follows us to work over the Internet. It titillates 24/7. Nonetheless, there are preventive measures that hold real promise. You don't have to be hooked by this easy temptation. And if you are already hooked, I have a specific prescription for you in just a moment. First, I offer just one simple suggestion for the man who is not compulsive about viewing porn, but knows it is an ever-present temptation.

Are you ready? Here it is: Be a man. I don't mean this as glibly as it sounds. I mean it with all sincerity, and it's one of the best means I know for protecting yourself against the temptation of pornography.

> *Marriage provides the greatest possibility for intimacy because it is predicated on the idea of exclusivity.*
> **Francine Klagsbrun**

What I'm getting at is that you've got to work hard to establish your maleness in a healthy way — without the cultural distortions of sexual promiscuity. Why? Because ultimately, pornography lures you into its clutches with enticements of women who are ready to be used in your fantasy. But pornography inevitably cheats you from being with your fantasy women and inexorably causes you to feel unmanly as a result. It's a psychological reality. So don't take the bait.

Instead, stand strong and continually ask God to help you set your sights on being a man who walks tall, a man of character and confidence. Focus on qualities like bravery, strength of purpose, honesty, integrity, kindness, loyalty. Pray earnestly to be a man who embodies these attributes. Ask God to help you exercise manly control over your sexual impulses, not relying on the temporary fix of ejaculating over an image on a computer screen or magazine. Only men who lack these qualities do so in order to exert their feeble masculinity.

A real man's expression of his sexuality is to be respectful of himself and of his wife. "Mature sexuality is relational," says psychiatrist Louis McBurney, "not regressively self-focused. Men who feel good about their strength don't have to escape from reality."

I'm not knocking practical things you can do like put an Internet filter on your computer that prevents easy access to porn. You should do that if needed. And I'm certainly not neglecting a support group of other men who can help keep you on the straight and narrow. I strongly encourage it, and I participate in one myself. But I simply want to drive home the point that the most powerful stance you can take against being hooked by porn is to ask God to help you be man enough to resist it.

Protecting Yourself against Porn — If You're Already Hooked

One of the saddest things I ever see in my counseling office is a man who has hit bottom because of an untreated pornography addiction. Men in this situation end up seeing me because their marriage is falling apart, and they are desperate to end an addiction that has generally been going on in isolation for years.

I don't know if this is you or not, but I can tell you

that if you are deep into a dependency upon porn, you can turn it around. You don't have to let it control you. The methods explained below are proven ways of getting men to battle this problem successfully. I offer them to you with a sense of urgency, knowing that the sooner you get started, the sooner you'll get your life back. But I also offer them to you knowing that this is a process. Pornography addiction is not a quick-fix. So at the end of my suggestions, I'll point you to some reputable places for going deeper and getting the personalized help you really need.

Confess Carefully

A major issue for most guys in moving beyond an addiction to porn is their ambivalence. One moment, they may deeply yearn never to use it again, only to run back to it quickly in the next. Like a person attempting to quit smoking, they just can't keep their commitment to stop. That's why confession is a helpful first step. It gets you off the fence of ambivalence. Chances are, you've never told anyone about your personal struggle. So once you've confessed it to God, confess it to a brother in Christ who will hold your confession carefully and confidentially.

> *The negative effects of pornography have been more consistently proven than the links between smoking and lung cancer.*
>
> **Dr. Dolf Zillman**

So think this through carefully. Who can you confide in? Who will support you and pray for you? That's who you want to tell. Make it intentional. Set up a time to meet and follow through. Oh, but don't do so just because I'm suggesting it. A true confession is never coerced.

Remember the story of the woman caught in adultery (John 8:2 – 11)? One morning, while Jesus was teaching in the courtyard of the temple, a group of Pharisees and teachers of the law came in, bringing a woman with them. "Teacher, this woman was caught in the act of adultery," they said. "In the law Moses commanded us to stone such women. Now what do you say?"

There was deathly silence. Everyone waited to hear his answer. Jesus knew they were trying to trick him: if he said to stone her, he would be disobeying the Roman law, which forbade carrying out the death sentence. But if he told them not to stone her, he would be disobeying God's law. Jesus bent down and wrote in the sand. When the men continued to pester him, he said, "If any one of you is without sin, let him be the first to throw a stone at her."

The angry little mob fell silent and stole away, one by one. The woman and Jesus were left standing together.

"Woman, where are they? Has no one condemned you?" he asked her.

"No one, sir."

Jesus brushed the dirt from his hands. "Then neither

do I condemn you," he told her. "Go now, and leave your life of sin."

I've often wondered if Jesus really meant to say that. I mean, shouldn't he have gotten her to promise to change *before* pronouncing his forgiveness? That's how most of us think. But that's not Christ's way of responding to guilt. Jesus did not want a coerced confession motivated by fear. He wanted her to *choose* a better way of living in order to *be* a better person. And that's exactly what he wants for you. And it begins when your heart is ready to confess it. So consider confessing to another man in your life, a trusted and caring man, a man who will help you stay accountable on a regular basis. This needs to be a man who understands the struggle and genuinely cares about you as a follower of Christ — not simply someone who will "police" you without godly wisdom.

> *Shut out all of your past except that which will help you weather your tomorrows.*
>
> **Sir William Osler**

Revel in God's Mercy

Every man I've treated with an addiction to pornography falsely believes he must do something to earn God's favor. As a result these men wallow in feelings of guilt that get them nowhere.

Paul, who was "sorrowful, yet always rejoicing," understood this (2 Corinthians 6:10). So did Martin Luther, eventually. When he was still a Catholic monk, he struggled with unbounded feelings of guilt. He meticulously observed all the requirements of his religious order and confessed his sins repeatedly. He was so obsessed with confessing even the minutest sins that once his superior chided him. "If you expect God to forgive you, come in to confession with something to forgive!"

When we relate to God out of a guilty conscience, we try to earn our worth by being severely critical of ourselves. Rather than relying on God's mercy, we struggle to show God how good we are. A sense of inadequacy drives us to prove that we are deserving of God's forgiveness.

But you'll only experience God's forgiveness when you quit trying to earn it. When Martin Luther came across Romans 1:17, "the righteous will live by faith," he saw the futility of all his good works. For the first time, he recognized how useless it was to try to earn God's acceptance, and he rested in the gift of God's amazing grace. His decision to base his life on faith changed his life and revolution-

> *It's ruining marriages, destroying relationships, harming youth, and hurting the body of Christ. You hardly need to be reminded that fallen pastors and priests did not "suddenly" fall. More often than not, pornography played a role in their downward spiral.*
>
> **Chuck Swindoll**

ized the church. The same kind of faith will revolutionize your heart and help you win the battle against porn.

If you sincerely ask God for forgiveness, you can be confident you are forgiven. "If we confess our sins," Scripture tells us, "he is faithful and just and will forgive us our sins" (1 John 1:9).

Go Deep for Personalized Help and Accountability

The suggestions I've provided here are only a start. To successfully battle your addiction to porn, if that's the place you are in, you're going to need a personalized plan of attack. And you're going to need support and accountability. Everyone involved in any kind of recovery from any kind of addiction will tell you that you can't go it alone. You've got to have others who walk beside you — some who have already journeyed the same road and serve as guides, and some who are walking it for the first time just like you.

The list of helpful organizations and resources on pages 194 – 95 is designed to help you do exactly that. I'm providing you with a list of organizations, their primary location, and their website. Most of them have a network of support that you can find in your own community. I urge you to explore each of them and find a resource that you feel will best help you in this healing process.

Now's the Time

I want to leave you with a final thought, a story, actually, as you journey toward a new life, free of pornography addiction. Whether you are protecting yourself before you get hooked or especially if you already are, this story is for you.

It's the story of a mythical golf match set in 1930s Savannah, Georgia, involving golf legends Bobby Jones, Walter Hagen, and hometown ace Rannulph Junuh. You may know the story as *The Legend of Bagger Vance*, a Robert Redford film starring Will Smith and Matt Damon.

As a teenager, Junuh (Damon) had tremendous promise as a golfer. But after his World War I tour of duty, he is marred psychologically and loses interest in golf. Content to gamble and drink, Junuh is a recluse until his former girlfriend invites him to join Jones and Hagen in an exhibition match. During the exhibition match, with four holes to play in the final round, Junuh successfully overcomes his several strokes deficit and takes a two-stroke lead. But by the sixteenth hole, he trails again. On the seventeenth hole, he slices his tee shot deep into the woods. As he enters the dark forest to find his ball, panic overtakes him. The steam evaporating

Men's use of porn distracts them from the task of trying to please their real-life partners.

Aline Zoldbrod

from the ground triggers memories of smoking battle-fields where he watched all his company die. His hands tremble and he drops his clubs. Upon finding his ball, he calls it quits. He remembers why he quit playing golf and started drinking. Just then, Bagger (Smith), his golfing mentor, finds him and asks which club he'd like from his bag. He proceeds to tell Junuh that his problems have to do with the grip the past holds on him.

"Ain't a soul on this entire earth ain't got a burden to carry he don't understand," Bagger consoles in the film. "You ain't alone in that. But you been carryin' this one long enough. Time to go on. Lay it down."

Junuh admits, "I don't know how."

Bagger replies, "You got a choice. You can stop, or you can start."

"Start?"

"Walking."

"Where?"

"Right back to where you always been and then stand there. Still, real still. And remember."

"It's too long ago."

"Oh no, son. It was just a moment ago. Time for you to come on out of the shadows, Junuh. Time for you to choose."

"I can't," Junuh protests.

"Yes, you can," Bagger counters. "But you ain't alone. I'm right here with you. I've been here all along. Now play the game. Your game. The one that only you was meant to play. The one that was given to you when you come into this world. You ready? Take your stance. Strike that ball, Junuh. Don't hold nothin' back. Give it everything. Now's the time ..."

And now is your time. Your past has held a grip on you for too long. You've been carrying regrets and guilt long enough. It's time to lay them down. In the pages of this book, I've done my best to show you exactly how to do just that. Like Junuh, you now have a choice. You can hold on to your guilt and regret, or you can come out of the shadows of your past and fulfill your destiny.

It's your choice. I just have a couple of quick reminders. First, you are not alone. God walks with you, giving grace at every step. Second, the tragedy of life is not that it ends so soon, but that we wait so long to begin it. Don't waste another day being pulled down by pornography.

Now's the time.

For Reflection

1. What and when was your first exposure to porn and how did it make you feel?

2. Personally speaking, when are you most tempted to access pornography and why?

3. What is one practical thing you can do — starting immediately — to deter yourself from accessing pornography? What keeps you from implementing it?

 Check this out! You'll find a special online video feature specifically designed to augment what you have just read in this chapter, along with a message from Dr. Parrott. Go to **CrazyGoodSex.jLog.com/Ch5** to find the jLog for Myth 3.

A Note to the Curious Woman
about Porn

I know. Pornography makes you sick and the mere thought that your husband would be interested in seeing it is beyond your understanding. But if you could sit in my counseling office and listen to the brokenhearted men cry out to be free from the bondage of pornography, you might have a clearer understanding of just how powerful porn can be for some men. It really is every bit as addictive as a drug. Of course, not all men are drawn to it intensely or compulsively. But every man I've ever met has had to at least occasionally fight off the impulse to indulge such an accessible evil.

What can you do to help? First of all, you need to be willing to talk — without condemnation — about the reality of this struggle for men. Why? Because if you pretend the temptation doesn't exist for your man, you increase the chances of driving him to struggle in secrecy. And that only compounds the problem. Of course, this doesn't mean you need to continually bring the issue of pornography up to him. That is definitely not helpful. He doesn't want to feel like he's married to the porn police. It simply means being willing to have an adult conversation with him about the reality of this temptation. Also, don't expect to keep your husband accountable on this issue. Not everyone may agree with me on this, but in my experience with couples who are grappling with this issue, I've found that accountability is better handled by a mentor or a friend. When a wife attempts to play this role, it too often ends up in an unproductive game of cat and mouse with him going online and attempting to cover his tracks, then your intuition telling you that "something is going on," followed by bickering that goes nowhere.

If you are particularly concerned about your husband's online surfing, I recommend that you both explore the installation of an Internet filter or monitoring software. This eliminates the need for you to play Nancy Drew, and it serves as a constant reminder to your husband that he's not surfing in private.

Size Matters

The totally unrealistic expectation or misconception is that to be a good lover, a guy has to have a humongous penis and an erection you can strike matches on.

Sue Johanson

A professor stands in front of a class and asks an anatomy student what organ in the human body expands to ten times its normal size when excited. The blushing and flustered female student responds that it's inappropriate for the professor to be asking her such questions, to which the professor replies, with a glint of mirth: "Well we've learned three things so far:

"You've got a lot to learn about the human anatomy — I was referring of course to the iris of the human eye, you've got a dirty mind, and you're likely to be very disappointed."

You've probably heard this joke before. It's been around for a while. But it embodies a misnomer this chapter is dedicated to correcting. Truth be told, it is the male that is likely to be disappointed, not the female. Why? Because it is men – not women – who are seemingly obsessed with the size of their "manhood."

The first ruler was invented in 1675, and I'm guessing that before 1676 some guy had used it to measure his penis. You've probably done the same thing. Most likely in your adolescence when you first noticed it was getting bigger, or maybe later when you noticed everyone else's *was* big and yours wasn't. At some point almost every guy measures himself – and rounds up to the nearest half-inch – if only as an act of reassurance.

To the average man, his penis is, consciously or subconsciously, one of the most important things in the world. At an early age he discovers it and immediately becomes fascinated by it. But then a bit of uncertainty enters his mind: Isn't mine rather small? Look at Dad's, look at big brother's, look at those in the men's changing room. He asks himself if he will be as big as that. And so he goes through life, always a tiny bit sensitive about the size of his organ, always convinced that it would be nicer if it were just a little bit bigger.

For millennia, men the world over have been obsessed with penis size. Sly jokes, furtive glances in the locker room, and wildly exaggerated claims of endowment suggest that "penis envy" is a decidedly male trait. With apologies to Dr. Freud, it's true. In fact, many sex experts report that the size of a man's penis is the number-one source of his sexual anxiety.

Even in this supposedly enlightened century, men fret about penis size. Though the vast majority of guys have more than enough bulk to perform well with their wives, a widespread masculine obsession that "more would be better" prevails. Given the society we live in, where a man's worth is measured by the size of everything from his car to his income to his penis, I suppose it's not surprising that many men think that size matters. But does it really? This notion is almost always misguided.

> *If you have only two inches, that's all you need to please a woman.*
>
> **Cliff and Joyce Penner**

No matter how often it's written that penile size doesn't matter and that women aren't attracted to a man because of the length of his organ, the average male continues to think otherwise. It's another example of men and "crazy sex." And it's time you put this crazy myth to bed once and for all.

In an effort to help you do just that, I'm going to tell you exactly how you measure up by revealing what scientists and doctors say is "average." From there we'll get into the honest reasons why bigger isn't better — and what you should do about the size of your penis.

Average Joe

For as long as there have been measuring tools, men
have been wondering how they rate. Even the following snippet of conversation between two literary greats
underscores the obsessive insecurity: "There's nothing
wrong with you. You look at yourself from above and you
look foreshortened," Hemingway reassured a panicking
F. Scott Fitzgerald. "It is basically not a question of the
size in repose. It is the size that it becomes. It is also a
question of angle."

Angle, schmangle! Men want to know how they
compare to what's average. The answer is not as easy
as you might guess. The trouble occurs because most
of the actual surveys of penis size are unscientific and
unreliable.

Since March of 1995, Richard Edwards, a pseudo-
science-minded Canadian, has been attempting to dissect
penis fact from phallic fallacy. To this end, he has created
"The Definitive Penis Size Survey" which attempts to de-
mystify that part of the male anatomy which often pro-
duces either extreme pride or provokes intense anxiety.
According to Edwards, the average penis length is five
inches when limp — and six when erect. But, again, this is
not, ahem, hard science (pardon the pun).

Perhaps the most famous and oft-quoted "scientific"
study was conducted by Alfred Kinsey in the fifties and

sixties. Kinsey provided 3,500 subjects with postcards against which they were to mark the maximum extent of their erection. About 2,500 men responded and the average turned out to be 6.25 inches in length. Another study using similar methodology in 1996 got similar results (6.38 inches).

The problem here is what has become known as "self-reportage bias." Even when assured that the results are completely anonymous, guys tend to exaggerate. You'd think it would be the opposite. That they'd deliberately *under*estimate the size of their penises in order to skew down the average size to which they would then compare themselves more favorably. Self-reportage bias is a real phenomenon and has been observed in numerous surveys on everything from drinking habits to stated income. In fact, a whole school of statistical analysis has developed on how to adjust for this bias.

Love is an irresistible desire to be irresistibly desired.

Robert Frost

The Kinsey survey relied on men to report their own numbers honestly and accurately—never a good idea. Since then, there have been numerous attempts to settle on a number: from various Web surveys to the condom company that did a survey in Cancun during spring break.

However, reliable data is finally emerging. Tom Lue, MD, a urologist at the University of California in San Francisco, has compiled a survey of a diverse group of male subjects to determine average penis size. Dr. Lue's research measured circumference and length in both limp and erect penises and asked participants questions. The results indicated that what men frequently consider small is actually the norm. Lue found the average limp penis measured 3.5 inches, while the average erect length reached 5.1 inches. Limp circumference averaged 3.9 inches and average erect circumference came to 4.9 inches. So there you have it. The average penis size is, well, pretty average.

What Determines Size?

Now if you are really concerned about your penis size as it relates to a national average, you should probably know exactly what, biologically speaking, determines the size of an erect penis. Why? Because it has a direct implication on whether your penis can become larger.

The size of the penis is a direct function of the capacity of the *tunica albuginea*, a tough fibrous sheath that surrounds the *corpus cavernosum*. The following diagram will make all this Latin clearer.

Once the tunica albuginea is maxed out, that's it. You're only ever going to be as big as that biological apparatus allows. Interestingly, most penises are very much the same size when erect. The man whose non-erect penis is smallish will usually achieve about a 100 percent

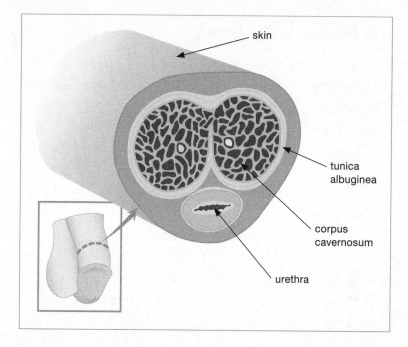

increase in length during sexual excitement. The man whose non-erect penis is on the largish size will probably manage about a 75 percent increase.

This means the great majority of penises measure a bit over five inches when erect. So you can see that even if a man has a "small" penis, he's got a built-in compensating factor that will bring him up to about the same size as the guy who appears to be "better equipped" when not erect. While most men seem to have either one that "shows" or one that "grows," in both cases the size of their erection is very similar.

Is Bigger Really Better?

Of course, it's true that some men have big penises and some have smaller ones, just as some men have small feet and some have big feet, but the measurement is not—repeat, *not*—an index of virility. You've probably heard the juvenile sayings about male endowment, or lack thereof, as it relates to pleasing a woman:

"It's not how long your pencil is—it's how you write your name."

"It's not the wand—it's the magician."

And then there's the popular, "It's not the size of the boat—it's the motion of the ocean."

But are these sentiments true? Is there anything to back up the idea that bigger isn't really better—that it's how you use what you have? I'm devoting this section to finding out. More honestly, I'm devoting it to the fact that what you believe about penis size as it relates to your wife's sexual satisfaction and what your wife believes, in all likelihood, are two very different things.

Why?

Because, if you're like most men, you don't know jack about her vagina. Virtually every man forgets that it doesn't matter how long or how short his penis is, because his wife's vagina will accommodate itself to any length. The vagina of a woman who hasn't had a child is only about 7.5 cm (3 inches) long when she's not sexually excited. The figures for women who have had babies are only slightly different. Even when aroused, a woman's vagina usually extends only to a length of about 10 cm (4 inches).[1] This means that virtually any man's penis will fill a vagina completely.

By the way, if you're still thinking bigger is better, say hello to this little known fact: During intercourse, the tip of a long penis can strike a woman's cervix and cause pain for a woman. You're probably now wondering how the average man with an erection of six inches manages to insert his penis into the vagina at all. Well, the vagina has the most remarkable capacity for lengthening if something is introduced into it gradually. So the exceptionally large man whose erect penis is eight inches long can still make love to his wife, providing he excites her properly and introduces his organ very slowly. If he does this, her vagina will lengthen by 150 to 200 percent to accommodate him.

The vagina is an organ of accommodation and penis size has nothing to do with masculinity or sexual competence.

Cliff and Joyce Penner

But here's the most important point that most men don't recognize: Your wife's most sensitive nerves in her vagina are located close to the opening of it — the outer one-third. That's right. There is little sexual stimulation that happens as a result of a large penis, because the nerves near the opening of the vagina are the most sensitive to sexual stimulation. In fact, even a penis that is fully erect at just two inches would be enough to achieve sexual satisfaction for her! According to Joy Davidson, PhD, author of *Fearless Sex*, bigger isn't better because, as she tells women, "a small penis tends to fit nicely against your G-spot, whereas a larger one can miss it entirely."

> *Sex is like snow;*
> *you never know*
> *how many inches*
> *you're going to*
> *get or how long it*
> *will last.*
>
> **Unknown**

Okay, so maybe you have insecurities about your size even if it does satisfy your wife. Maybe you think a small penis will be a physical turnoff. Well, it might surprise you, but your wife is not very much interested in looking at your anatomy — not even close to the way you like looking at hers. Ninety percent of women having intercourse, even if it is dark, prefer to close their eyes. So they are not interested in looking at the size of your penis. Plus, once your wife has been satisfied during intercourse, even if your penis is not setting any size records, she is not going to be bothered about its size.

As if that wasn't enough, most men also don't take into account that a woman's primary sexual pleasure is found outside of the vagina. Men mistakenly believe that intercourse is what gives women sexual pleasure. If that were the case, perhaps a bigger penis would give more pleasure. But it's not the case. In fact, it's just plain wrong. Intercourse gives men tremendous pleasure, and most women enjoy it too. But the main organ of women's sexual pleasure is not the vagina, but the clitoris, which sits outside of it and above it, under the place where the vaginal lips meet.

Are you following all of this? *The size of your penis has next to nothing to do with your ability to satisfy your wife's sexual needs. Period.* So why do you still feel as though you should be bigger? Allow me to make a suggestion.

What to Do about Your Penis Size

Comedian Mike Myers wrote, produced, and starred in a series of three films about Austin Powers, a British spy in the sixties. The series, in part, spoofed the James Bond franchise, poking fun at the outrageous plots and rampant sexual innuendos of the one-dimensional character. In one scene from the first film, Austin Powers is caught denying the ownership of his penis enlarger pump. A clerk presents Austin with a crushed-velvet suit, a pair of pointy black boots, a silver medallion, and finally the enlarger:

CLERK: One Swedish-made penis enlarger.

AUSTIN POWERS: That's not mine.

CLERK: One credit card receipt for Swedish-made penis enlarger signed by Austin Powers.

AUSTIN POWERS: I'm telling ya, baby, that's not mine.

CLERK: One warranty card for Swedish-made penis enlarger pump, filled out by Austin Powers.

AUSTIN POWERS: I don't even know what this is! This sort of thing ain't my bag, baby.

CLERK: One book, *Swedish-made Penis Enlarger Pumps and Me: This Sort of Thing Is My Bag Baby*, by Austin Powers.

Myers calls this line of dialogue in his film "comic torture," because it takes a joke much farther than it should go. Comedic torture, he says, comes from repeating something until it stops being funny and then repeating it some more until it becomes funny again.

Well, everyone has a different sense of humor and whether or not you find his method funny or not, I can assure you that you don't ever have to torture yourself with any kind of penis enlarger.

Contrary to the unsolicited junk emails you receive, not to mention the ads on sports radio shows for pumps, pills, weights, and exercises, these gimmicks and devices simply will not enlarge your penis. But, you may be thinking to yourself, they have to do something in order to stay in business. Yes, they promote stereotypes about men's insecurities in order to sell you a "miracle solution" that does nothing. That's it. It's kind of like pills that make you instantly lose weight. If they really worked miracles, would anyone still be obese?

None of the products that you see or hear advertised for penis enlargement work. None of them. You cannot increase the size of your penis with pills, pumps, or exercises. So please don't waste your money. But I can tell you the secret to making the most of what the good Lord gave you. No matter whether it's flaccid or erect, the size of your penis depends on the amount of blood contained in the organ. So if you want to be as large as you possibly can be, you'll want to make sure that you have excellent blood flow – good circulation – there.

There's a new medical crisis. Doctors are reporting that many men are having allergic reactions to latex condoms. They say they cause severe swelling. So what's the problem?

Dustin Hoffman

What can you do to ensure this? First, if you smoke, stop! I have a friend who says we could probably eradicate smoking in this country among men if the government bought billboards that said, "Your Penis Shrinks with Every Puff." Actually, this is medically true. Smoking accelerates the narrowing of arteries, which is why smoking is a major risk factor for heart attack. Smoking also narrows the two arteries that carry blood into the penis. So the more you smoke, the less blood gets into your penis, and the smaller you look. So first and foremost, don't smoke.

Secondly, relax about this. Most men notice that in a

cold locker room their penises shrivel up, but when they step into a hot shower, they feel more like a man. That's because the hot water of a shower is relaxing. When men relax, the arteries that carry blood into the penis also relax; they open up and more blood flows into the organ. So the irony of men's anxiety about penis size is the more you worry about it, the smaller it gets.

Finally, if you're overweight, lose weight. When a man gets a big gut, a pad of fat develops in the lower abdomen and tends to cover the base of his penis. So your penis doesn't shrink, but it does look smaller. If you want to look bigger, lose the gut.

The bottom line? Stop worrying already. Your penis is fine.

I receive a number of questions via email from men and women who visit RealRelationships.com. Because my wife, Leslie, and I actually record video answers to the questions people write in, we have a steady stream of questions — daily. And many of them are about sex. But not once has a woman ever written in, saying, "My husband's penis is too small; I wish it were bigger." Not one woman has ever said this. Several newlywed women have written in, saying, "My husband is too big, and I'm afraid he's going to hurt me with it."

As far as phallic symbols go, the penis has only half a foot to stand on. And that's a stretch.

Anonymous

Hundreds of women have written in saying, "My husband's penis is perfectly fine; why is he so obsessed with this nonsense that he's too small?" But *never* a woman asking how her husband's penis could be bigger.

Still Not Convinced?

Before I close this chapter, I've got to tell you about one last study. It found that sex education among men concerned about small penis size is very successful at relieving men of their anxiety about the matter.[2] In other words, the information you've read in this chapter is very likely to correct your misguided beliefs and help eliminate your unnecessary concerns.

That's the good news.

But the study also found that for a small percentage of men this type of sex education does not lower their personal anxiety on the matter. In fact, this minority of men suffer from a newly proposed diagnosis called "Small Penis Syndrome." It occurs when a man's anxiety about the matter is still not lessened despite being shown that he does not have an unusually small penis.

The study, published in the journal *Urology*, was conducted by the Cairo University Hospital Department of Andrology and Sexology. Over two years, it focused on 92 patients complaining of a small-sized penis in either the flaccid or erect state. None of the patients had erectile dysfunction.

The doctors found that almost all of the patients had an inflated concept of what size a normal penis should be. Their anxiety about their penis size did not diminish with education alone, however. It also required tangible measurements. In other words, these patients said they did not find relief from their anxiety until they actually performed a measurement of themselves. And, according to the study, almost all the patients were incorrect in what they thought to be normal penile size. Once their measurements were done, *all* of the patients were relieved to find they did not have an undersized penis.

> *For patients with psychological concern about the size of the penis — particularly if it is normal size — there is little point in offering them surgery because it makes no difference.*
>
> **Nim Chistopher**

The implication? I think you get it. So, if at this point you still suffer from Small Penis Syndrome, find a ruler and do what you have to do.

For Reflection

1. When did you first become concerned about your penis size? If you haven't, why not? When did you become aware of the fact that most guys suffer from anxiety or concern about their penis size?

2. On a scale of one to ten, how concerned do you believe your wife (or if you are single, your future wife) is about the size of your penis? Why?

3. If you were a counselor, what advice would you give to another guy who seems to suffer from too much concern about the size of his penis?

 Check this out! You'll find a special online video feature specifically designed to augment what you have just read in this chapter, along with a message from Dr. Parrott. Go to CrazyGoodSex.jLog.com/Ch6 to find the jLog for Myth 4.

A Note to the Curious Woman
about Penis Size

Chances are this topic isn't that important to you — and you're wondering why it might be important to your husband (a little more than half of all men have worried about their penis size). Well, there's no need for you to play Dr. Freud on this topic. Just accept the fact that your husband may be sensitive about not being bigger. Even if he doesn't admit it, he may have a bit of concern at a deeper level. So, by all means, never joke about him being small. It's not a joking matter. It's humiliating to a man. Just as there are certain topics that are off-limits for you (like maybe your weight) when it comes to joking around, this is one to stay clear of with him.

Instead, make sure your husband knows how much he pleases you (the more specific the better). Don't take it for granted. Let him know that he makes you feel good. Of course, don't make this up or lie about it. If there's a problem with you achieving genuine pleasure for any reason, you'll want to seek the advice of your gynecologist or physician or a sexual therapist. In all likelihood it has absolutely nothing to do with his penis size. So don't hold back on your affirmation of his efforts on your behalf in the bedroom.

The Bible Is Very Clear on Masturbation

Some say masturbation is an outright sin because it looks and feels like sin. But remember that Satan is a master of deception, specializing in decoys.

Steve Gerali

In my book *Helping Your Struggling Teenager*, I explore thirty-six common issues that young people struggle with, such as peer pressure, depression, video game addiction, sibling rivalry, and so on. And among the chapters I have one that is dedicated to masturbation. As a result, I occasionally have a magazine editor call and ask me to write an article on the subject. In fact, some time ago a popular magazine for youth pastors asked me to do just that.

A few weeks later, after submitting my article, I received an envelope at my university office from the magazine. It was my paycheck for writing the article. I separated the check from the perforated pay stub and placed it in my wallet. Then I looked more carefully at the pay stub. It read: "Dr. Les Parrott, Masturbation, $150."

I'm guessing you've never received a check like that, right?

I chuckled to myself as I set the stub on the corner of my desk and proceeded to thumb through the rest of my mail. Just then, one of my fellow professors from down the hallway stepped into my office. We began talking about course schedules, but in mid-sentence, the professor stopped. Wide-eyed, he studied the paystub on my desk, looked up at me, back at the pay stub, and then said, "Les, you get *paid* for that?"

Not exactly.

But I've counseled enough men over the years to know that if they were getting paid for this behavior, many would be able to quit their full-time jobs.

> *We have reason to believe that man first walked upright to free his hands for masturbation.*
>
> **Lily Tomlin**

Mark Driscoll, pastor of the growing megachurch in Seattle, Mars Hill, is only half-joking when he tells of a guy in his congregation trying to justify masturbation by quoting Ecclesiastes 9:10, a passage plainly referring to vocation, which says, "Whatever your hand finds to do, do it with all your might."[1]

Few sexual behaviors have caused more confusion,

consternation, and crazy thinking for the man who wants to live free from "sexual immorality" (1 Corinthians 6:18) than masturbation. I have counseled more men troubled by masturbation (especially married men) than any other sexual problem. It's been said for years, "Masturbation is one of the most frequently discussed, most roughly condemned, and most universally practiced forms of sexual behavior." From ancient times to the present, no sexual practice seems to have been more controversial than masturbation. In the 1800s, abstinence from this kind of "self-abuse" was lauded as crucial to health. The Reverend Sylvester Graham, a contemporary of John Harvey Kellogg (noted in chapter 1), invented a cracker to help men curb their inclinations to masturbate. And like Dr. Kellogg's Corn Flakes, Graham's cracker lives on to this day because of its flavor—not because it is a medicinal means to curtail masturbation. In his writings, *Lectures to Young Men on Chastity*, Graham beseeched men to abstain from masturbation "to avoid a reduction in health-reserving vital fluids and to avoid moral and physical degeneracy."[2]

In a 1918 *Encyclopedia of Health and Home*, one could find this tidbit about those "addicted to the habit" of

> *Subjecting our genitals to oppression has made them subject to compulsions, and compulsions do not satisfy.*
> **James B. Nelson**

masturbation: "Few ever know how many of the unfortunate inmates of our lunatic asylums have been sent there by this dreadful vice."[3]

Like I said at the start, there's a lot of *crazy* thinking — quite literally in this case — about sexuality.

Now you may be thinking that these kinds of beliefs are remnants of century-old attitudes no longer found in contemporary culture. But don't be too sure. You'll find modern Christians purporting that masturbation is more dangerous than smoking. Some say it's more dangerous than AIDS. That it causes forgetfulness. It results in nearsightedness.[4] That it causes the genitals to lose their form, or wear out early. You'll hear some say that people who masturbate often become impotent or frigid. Of course, these are not the most mainstream of attitudes within the church, but masturbation still remains a source of crazy thinking. And even for the most reasoned among us, masturbation is often viewed as a sinful behavior clearly prohibited and condemned in the Bible.

But is it really? Is the Bible explicit and plain on this subject? Does it offer a definitive truth and a clear directive? Does it flatly condemn masturbation with no exceptions? Does it state that it is entirely off-limits — end of discussion? You'd be hard-pressed to find a Bible scholar who would say so, which is why I dedicate this chapter to debunking the myth that the Bible is clear about masturbation.

Let's take a look at the facts.

How Common Is Masturbation?

It has long been reported that 98 percent of men masturbate and the remaining 2 percent are liars. Of course this is said tongue-in-cheek. But is it true? Does every man on the planet masturbate?

Reliable research reveals that over 90 percent of males and 50 percent of females have masturbated to orgasm at some point in their lives. And while some research reports that women tend to learn about masturbation over the entire life cycle, the onset of masturbation for men appears to be an adolescent experience, with 80 percent of males masturbating by about age 15.[5]

> *A sexually repressive upbringing creates excessive guilt around sexual feelings, and this sets up the obsessive need for masturbation.*
>
> **Dr. Archibald Hart**

In a survey of the sex lives of Christian men conducted by Dr. Archibald Hart, Hart found that almost all (96 percent) males under age 20 masturbate regularly, and the average number of times per month was fourteen. He also found that this is about the same for most married men in his sample as well. In other words, the frequency of masturbation in males remains relatively consistent from adolescence through adulthood. Teenage boys masturbate with no more frequency than most adult men.[6]

Another famous study of sexual behavior known as "The Janus Report" found that 24 percent of males under age 26 masturbate daily or several times a week. From age 27 to 38 it is 28 percent; from 39 to 50 it is 23 percent; over 50, 32 percent.[7] The habit of masturbation, it seems, is established early and continues throughout a man's life.

You may be wondering if this is true for men that are married. Well, in Dr. Hart's survey he found that 61 percent of married Christian men still masturbate. That's three out of every five married men admitting to masturbating—and they report doing so between one and five times a month. About 10 percent reported an average of between five and ten times per month. Six percent confess to more than fifteen times a month.

So why do so many married men still masturbate? The most common reasons given are "I have a strong sex drive," and "I enjoy it." Some said it was because they had no other sexual outlet available to them because of a wife who was ill or because of travel that kept them away from their wife.

Why Some Say Masturbation Is So Bad

If masturbation is such a common experience, even among Christian men who are dedicated to their wives, why is it seen by some as so bad—even sinful?

After all, around the turn of the century, some adults were so against masturbation that they made their sons wear metal chastity belts at night that made it painful to have an erection. All kinds of chastity belts and other devices, in fact, were used to prevent masturbation, probably as far back in history as you can go. During the 1820s, some parents prevented male masturbation by piercing the foreskin with a wire and soldering the ends together. Masturbation was also discouraged with threats of blindness, madness, and illness.

Ann Landers said that you are addicted to sex if you have sex more than three times a day, and that you should seek professional help. I have news for Ann Landers: The only way I am going to get sex three times a day is if I seek professional help.

Jay Leno

Today, the most frequently cited arguments against masturbation, according to the *Baker Encyclopedia of Psychology*, include:

1. Only the immature person masturbates.

2. It is condemned in Scripture.[8]

3. Masturbation is unsocial or antisocial.

4. It violates the divinely intended purpose of sex.

5. It causes fatigue and physical debilitation.

6. It is a manifestation of low self-control.

7. The fantasies associated with masturbation are emotionally unhealthy.

8. It is sexually frustrating and not as satisfying as sex relations with a marital partner.

9. It is an indication of selfishness.

10. It leads to undesirable feelings like guilt and anxiety.[9]

Many experts see these arguments as being mostly oversimplified and even false. Still, the debate over masturbation is not settled. Ethical judgments about masturbation run all the way from viewing it as a sin more serious than fornication, adultery, or rape to placing it in the same category as head scratching.[10] Regardless of one's position on the subject,[11] it cannot be argued that masturbation among men or women is rare nor that it is always harmful, nor clearly against God's Word.

Masturbation and the Bible

Anyone who writes or speaks about masturbation is open to criticism. Why? Because Scripture does not address the issue directly. It doesn't prohibit it or encourage it. Without clear biblical guidance on this issue, we are left with a variety of conclusions and conflicting opinions. Masturbation is one of those "wisdom issues" where we must be careful not to judge others but remain faithful to our own understanding of biblical principles.

So where do you fall along the continuum? Do you see masturbation, in general, as something to be avoided at all costs because it goes against the will of God, or do you see it as not very important or serious as long as it's not causing other problems?

To help you determine for yourself where you stand, let me offer a few considerations.

First, let's consider masturbation from a medical or biological perspective. Every expert agrees that there is no scientific evidence to indicate that this act is harmful to the body. Despite terrifying warnings throughout history, it does not cause blindness, insanity, or any other physical problem.

Second, the Bible doesn't mention it. Let me be perfectly clear on this: *There are no verses in all of Scripture that speak directly to masturbation.* A few may still try to argue that the Old Testament account of Onan makes a clear point on masturbation. But it doesn't. When Onan's brother died, the custom was for Onan to impregnate his sister-in-law so she could have children to carry on his brother's name. Onan apparently wanted the inheritance for himself, so he practiced the withdrawal method of birth control: "But Onan knew that the offspring would not be his; so whenever he lay with his brother's wife, he spilled his semen on the ground to keep from producing offspring for his brother" (Genesis 38:9).

This passage was used until recent decades by some Christian groups who maintained that Onan's sin was actually masturbation. The term *"Onanism,"* in fact, was coined as a synonym of masturbation. This interpretation is no longer in common use since the passage clearly has nothing to do with masturbation. The technical term for what Onan did is called *coitus interruptus.*

So, once more, let's be clear: *The Bible doesn't talk about masturbation anywhere.* Period. Masturbation is not even mentioned, much less forbidden. This is a bit odd since masturbation is so common a human experience, and given that Scripture speaks of other sexual sins (some fairly perverse and rare) without any shyness at all. For whatever reason, we are left to more general biblical principles to guide us on this issue.

In addition, you may find it helpful to see the varying views espoused by committed and respected Christian leaders across the board. For example, on the prohibition side, Stephen Grunlan, in his book *Marriage and the Family: A Christian Perspective*, gives three reasons why Christians should avoid masturbation: First, there is no biological necessity for masturbation; second, masturbation is a solo act, and God created us as sexual beings to bring men and women together; third, the fantasies and thought life that accompany the act can be sinful.[12]

John Eldredge, in his popular book *Wild at Heart*, says, "Masturbation is sabotage. It is an inherently selfish act that tears you down." Southeastern Seminary Professor of ethics Daniel Heimbach, in *True Sexual Morality*, says, "I believe it is quite clear that solitary, non-relational, shallow, self-focused, nonproductive, one-dimensional, single-gender, self-stimulated sex opposes every positive moral characteristic revealed to be essential in God's design for sex. Self-stimulated sex may be less seriously outside God's design for sex than, say, physical adultery, or prostitution, or even sexual immodesty. But I believe we still must conclude that it is outside the biblical pattern and is therefore wrong."[13]

On the other hand, James Dobson, in his "Focus on the Family" film series, accepts masturbation as a normal part of growing up unless it becomes excessive. Charlie Shedd, in *The Stork Is Dead*, speaks of it as a "gift from God."[14] Christian therapist Dr. Douglas Rosenau, in his book *A Celebration of Sex*, says, "Mates who have never stimulated themselves have forfeited an opportunity to learn about their arousal patterns and what type of stroking feels best on which areas of their bodies."[15]

In *The Sexual Man*, Christian psychologist Archibald Hart says, "The secretiveness and privateness of masturbation will always remain, in my opinion, its most damaging aspect. And the more we condemn it, the more we keep it secret and private."[16] David Seamands of Asbury

Seminary says, "It's high time we stop making such a big deal of masturbation and give it the well-deserved unimportance it merits."[17]

So is there a definitive biblical "truth" about masturbation? Nope. Without a biblical directive we can't say it's always harmful. Of course, you might say that it is for you—but you have no grounds for casting judgment on the person who says it is not. Ultimately, we all need to decide for ourselves where we fall along the continuum.

Do you see masturbation, in general, as something to be avoided at all costs because it goes against the will of God for you, or do you see it as not very important or serious as long as it's not excessive and causing other problems? Do you see it as a gift from God or a tool of Satan? Wherever you land on this personal issue, it's important to note that this behavior can indeed lead to harm under certain circumstances.

When Masturbation Becomes Harmful

Most everyone would agree that masturbation can cross a line and become highly debilitating. It can become so harmful that it leads some men into a double life of deceit and debauchery. I've counseled enough men who have been ensnared by its harmful effects to see it up close. So let me point out three warning signs or hazards of masturbation.

When It Entails a Lifestyle of Lust

The most common concern about masturbation among Christians is that it involves lust. And Jesus clearly condemns lust: "But I tell you that anyone who looks at a woman lustfully has already committed adultery with her in his heart. If your right eye causes you to sin, gouge it out and throw it away. It is better for you to lose one part of your body than for your whole body to be thrown into hell" (Matthew 5:28 – 29). This leaves little doubt about the matter. Illicit sexual fantasies are clearly forbidden for any follower of Christ.

This raises the question, then, what is lust? Some define it as an intense and shameless craving for self-gratification. I like the way Frederick Buechner defines it: "Lust is the craving for salt of a person who is dying of thirst."[18] Insane, right? Crazy! Yet lust, for the leering man who indulges it, drives him to sinful and deadly places. "But each one is tempted when he is drawn away by his own desires and enticed. Then, when desire has conceived, it gives birth to sin; and sin, when it is full-grown, brings forth death" (James 1:14 – 15 NKJV).

> *It is with our passions as it is with fire and water; they are good servants but bad masters.*
>
> **Aesop**

In Scripture, lust typically means a strong desire that is sinful. And, of course, *sinful* is the key. After all, not all strong desires are sinful. You may have a strong desire to eat, but that's not sinful until it becomes gluttony (See Deuteronomy 21:20; 2 Corinthians 10:5; 2 Timothy 3:1 – 9; and 2 Peter 1:5 – 7).

In the same way, a strong sexual desire is not sin until it becomes a perversion of what God intended for you. After all, God created you to have sexual thoughts because he created you as a sexual being. These thoughts originate out of his design for us. It is normal, dare I say godly, to be aroused. God does not want us to repress our sexuality. But he does want us to manage it. That's why it is the amount of time, intensity, and priority we give to getting aroused that leads to lust.

And this is precisely why the issue requires discernment and is not universally one way for everyone. You can't tabulate lust. The Bible does not say that having ten sexual thoughts in a twenty-four-hour period, for example, equates to lusting. Ridiculous! Lust involves sexual thinking, but sexual thinking is not always lust.

"To give the impression that strong sexual urges and desires are always lust," says Steve Gerali in *The Struggle*, "is irresponsible." Steve, who has done more theological study and thoughtful consideration of this subject than anyone I know, goes on to say, "Making lust synonymous to masturbation — because as many have said, 'You can't do that without lusting' — is to superimpose a personal standard on all guys."

In other words, he is suggesting that one man's lust

may not be another man's lust. And he makes the point that sexual thoughts, desires, arousal, and even lust *precede* the need to masturbate. Masturbation, in a very real sense, is the *end* of lust, not the beginning. It serves as a way out of lust.

I have counseled numerous men whose work requires them to be away from their wife for extended periods, and they confess that masturbation keeps them faithful during these times of separation because it extinguishes their sex drive. Perhaps this is what Paul is getting at when he says, "No temptation has seized you except what is common to man, and God is faithful; he will not let you be tempted beyond what you can bear. But when you are tempted, he will also provide a way out, so that you can stand up under it" (1 Corinthians 10:13).

> *If masturbation were only a self-centered act of pleasure, it would not become as compulsive as it often is.*
>
> **Lewis B. Smedes**

Still, make no mistake, masturbation becomes harmful whenever it reinforces a lifestyle of unbridled lust. The Holy Spirit sheds light on this issue for each man, and only each man will know when he crosses the line from instinctual sexual thinking to the sin of sexual lust.

When It Becomes Compulsive

Masturbation has harmful implications when it becomes uncontrollable. This compulsivity occurs when the person is routinely preoccupied with sexual thoughts and fantasies leading to masturbation. The masturbatory behavior becomes ritualized. The person plans for it, even scheduling it into the routine of his day.

When masturbation becomes compulsive, the individual will take nearly any opportunity possible to masturbate. Just as a compulsive eater is fearful of not having access to food, this person is fearful of not having an opportunity to masturbate.

Perhaps the tell-tale indicator of this compulsivity is seen when the person has tried to curb his masturbating but is unable to. What's more, he continues his compulsive behavior in spite of negative consequences, such as not having sex with his wife, which he's probably denying or not perceiving.

It's important to note that sexually addictive behavior like this often displays a progressive increase in tolerance. In other words, the person needs ever-stronger "hits." Similar to a drug addict who needs more and more to feel the same high.

Similarly, the compulsive masturbator needs more and more of whatever behavior satisfied him in the past. Because this

Any habit which a boy has that causes this fluid to be discharged from the body tends to weaken his strength, to make him less able to resist disease.

The Boy Scouts of America, 1934

progression occurs over time, it's not always obvious. Initially, masturbation with fantasy was enough to satiate his sexual appetite. Later, he needs to view pornography while masturbating. This is then not enough, and he feels the need to actually meet someone. Suddenly, he realizes he's cruising at a bar or sex club, or going online to meet a sexual partner. It's difficult to exaggerate the harm masturbation can lead to when it becomes compulsive.

When It Becomes a Substitute for Real Sex

One of the most disheartening aspects of masturbation that I see in my counseling office is when a sex-starved couple enters the room because, knowingly or not, the husband's masturbation has become a substitution for healthy sexual relations with his wife. This, I believe, is what the apostle Paul meant when he instructed us not to "deprive" one another as marital partners: "Do not deprive each other except by mutual consent and for a time, so that you may devote yourselves to prayer. Then come together again so that Satan will not tempt you because of your lack of self-control" (1 Corinthians 7:5).

There are numerous reasons for a man to temporarily replace sex with his wife with sex by himself. It may be the result of extended illness, pregnancy, or repeated business travel, for example. Whatever the reason, it's a mere substitute. Sex was designed for enjoyment between a husband and his wife, and if masturbation is causing this important aspect of a marriage relationship to be snuffed out, it's not healthy, to say the least.

Guarding against Harmful Masturbation

The first time I ever remember hearing the term "masturbation" was when I was in the seventh grade. My parents gave me a set of audio tapes by renowned Christian psychologist Dr. James Dobson. It was called "Preparing for Adolescence." A couple of years later, my dad gave me a book by Tim Stafford called *A Love Story*. It also addressed masturbation. These two resources, early in my life, served a great purpose that I only discovered years later when I began my counseling practice as a psychologist.

They short-circuited, for me, the potential false guilt so many young men suffer from when it comes to masturbation. They helped me see that this was a normal human experience and that I wasn't some kind of adolescent sex freak. Research, by the way, indicates that masturbation decreases when any anxiety connected with it is alleviated.[19]

Am I saying that masturbation has never been a struggle for me? Of course not. But, thankfully, I've never wallowed in failure or inordinate feelings of guilt because of it. Mary Ann Mayo, in her book *A Christian Guide to Sexual Counseling*, says, "I have seen people invest forty-eight hours of self-wallowing condemnation and guilt as a result of four minutes of self-indulgent pleasure!"[20] I've seen the same thing in my counseling office.

So what's the secret? I believe it comes down to prayer and guidance from the Holy Spirit in deciding what's right for you and then learning how to become the master of your sexual impulses. I'm not here to build a case for or against masturbation in this chapter. As I said at the outset, this is a wisdom issue that requires you to come to a personal conclusion based on your own convictions. As the apostle Paul wrote, "But if anyone regards something as unclean, then for him it is unclean" (Romans 14:14).

If you've determined that masturbation is wrong for you, that it is sinful, and you're trying to control the practice as much as you possibly can, Stephen Grunlan offers these helpful suggestions: Avoid the time and places where masturbation has been practiced; avoid sexual stimuli in movies, television, music, or magazines; do not fight thoughts about masturbation, instead work at replacing them with other thoughts; take it one day at a time; and, finally, commit the matter to God in prayer.[21] It should be remembered, however, that the practice of masturbation is rarely ended by a direct determination to quit. This only seems to magnify the issue, increase anxiety, and make failure more incriminating. Still, Grunlan's suggestions are time-tested and have helped many. It's also helpful to consider what Steve Gerali says, "The struggle over masturbation can divert my focus from Christ even more than the act of masturbation."[22]

If, on the other hand, you have determined that masturbation is not a practice to be entirely squelched, you've got to remember the old camp meeting adage that you need to master your behavior, or else sin will master it for you. In other words, even if you don't believe that masturbation is a sin, if it is controlling you, then it becomes a sin. That's why Paul also wrote, "Everything is permissible for me — but not everything is beneficial. Everything is permissible for me — but I will not be mastered by anything" (1 Corinthians 6:12). Even a good thing can become sinful without the right heart. And certainly the amount of time, intensity, and priority you give to factors that create sexual arousal within you could make this behavior sinful whether you want to admit it or not.

The bottom line is that God made you to be a sexual being. If you try to repress your sexual nature, you're repressing a part of who God wants you to be. God gave you freedom. You are free to choose to engage in masturbation or not. And you are free to continually seek God's guidance on your choices as you continue to grow into the man he most wants you to be.

For Reflection

1. Does it make sense to you, from a biblical perspective, to call masturbation a "wisdom issue" that may lead different Christian men to believe different things about it? Why or why not?

2. If you were to counsel a young man about the issue of masturbation, what advice would you give him and why?

3. Under what conditions — if any — would you say that masturbation is permissible? Why?

 Check this out! You'll find a special online video feature specifically designed to augment what you have just read in this chapter, along with a message from Dr. Parrott. Go to CrazyGoodSex.jLog.com/Ch7 to find the jLog for Myth 5.

A Note to the Curious Woman
about Masturbation

As you already know, masturbation is generally less frequent among women than it is among men. And that may leave you wondering why your husband might find it to be such a struggle. And it may irritate you to think that on occasion he may actually find it more tempting to masturbate than to be with you. Your frustration here is understandable.

So what can you do about it? For starters, you can talk to him about it with a non-condemning attitude. In other words, you can invite him into a conversation about masturbation by letting him know you're genuinely interested in understanding what this issue is like for him. Now, don't expect him to immediately open up about it—and don't play the role of an investigative reporter peppering him with questions. After all, it's an uncomfortable topic and about as personal as it gets. But if and when he is willing, you might ask him how he first experienced it as a teenager. And be prepared to answer the same question yourself for him. The goal of the conversation is to simply better understand why masturbation is an issue most men, but your man specifically, have to contend with.

You may also want to talk together about some

of the points in this chapter — especially about the Bible's lack of content on the topic. And talk to him about the conditions, if any, that you would say masturbation is permissible. It is rare that a husband and wife have an honest and open conversation about this subject, but those who do find that their sex life improves. Why? Because, generally speaking, it helps the wife, in particular, to understand just how important it is for a man to have a sexual encounter with his wife on a regular basis. In other words, knowing about his potential struggle with masturbation just may be a motivator to be sure he's getting his sexual needs met with you. As one couple in a counseling session with me recently confessed, after they had an open conversation about it, she became much more agreeable to "a quickie" with him than ever before. And they both enjoyed a new aspect of their sexual relationship.

My Sex Drive Is
Too Powerful to Control

*See, the problem is that God gives men a brain
and a penis, and only enough blood to run one
at a time.*

Robin Williams

"A nimal instinct." It's a phrase we often hear in the context of human sexuality. But the person who uses it must know very little about the bizarre and kinky habits of the natural world. Consider the evidence. You've probably heard that the female praying mantis will bite the head off the male while they are mating. But have you heard that the lower half of the male will continue to copulate even after its top half has been consumed? And what should we make of the barbaric female sea worm, who abruptly turns on an unsuspecting male and munches the tail right off in order to fertilize her eggs? One more cannibalistic creature, just to make the point. The name of the black widow spider suggests death, but who'd have thought that she'd cold-bloodedly devour up to twenty-five mates in one day?

Not all the animal kingdom is so unpleasant. Many male species will go to great lengths to impress the females. That includes the most romantic of rodents, the mole rat, who painstakingly constructs not only an elaborate subterranean house of halls, but also a special "wedding chamber" exclusively reserved for mating. Then there's the female red-eyed tree frog, who carries her mate around on her back, then lifts him over the threshold and sets him gently down to fertilize her eggs.

Not to have control over the senses is like sailing in a rudderless ship, bound to break to pieces on coming in contact with the very first rock.

Mahatma Gandhi

As far as cats go, they do their business in the night with so much scratching and screeching that it makes sex sound about as appealing as being locked in a room with a manicurist who files fingernails on a chalkboard. Dogs are a lot less discreet. They are likely to do the deed at any time of day with any kind of thing. Maybe that's what some people mean by the natural "animal instinct" in men. They mean it's just involuntary, reflexive. We feel we have to "do it."

But do we? Is the sex drive in men so powerful that it's beyond our control? I've heard so many men propose this belief—the one echoed in comedian Robin Williams' quote at the opening—that I felt it deserved a chapter in this book. They argue that sexuality reveals our animal nature. It's a matter of biology, they say, of glands and hormones and physiological urgings that can't be curbed.

But is this true? Not if you tap into the power of your greatest sex organ.

Using Your Greatest Sex Organ

Bill Perkins, author of *When Good Men Are Tempted,* tells of having lunch with a friend on the day a story appeared in his local paper. "What did you think of the fire at Adult Fantasy Video?" he asked his friend. "I feel sorry for the guy who died," he added.

"Yeah, well, I feel sorry for his mother," I said. "Imagine having that be the last memory of your son."

"It could have been me," my buddy told me.

"What do you mean?" I asked, shocked.

"I've been in that place. I've been in that room," he said. "You could have been reading about me in the paper today and feeling sorry for my wife and kids."

"Are you ever going back?" I asked.

"I can't," he said. "It burned to the ground."

But the city slapped the owner's hand for a fire code violation, and his insurance company gave him a big enough settlement to rebuild.

A few weeks later Bill asked his friend if he'd visited the new store. He had. When Bill asked why, he said he didn't know. "Every time I leave that place, I feel like the scum of the earth. I swear I'll never go in there again. But later I just can't resist the urge. I'm caught and I can't get loose."

A common path to sexual sin is the notion that feelings are not only all-important but also totally uncontrollable; they just happen to you.

Louis McBurney, MD

Have you ever felt like this man? Be honest. It may not be an adult video store, but it may be a pornographic magazine or website. It may be a sexy blonde in your office who you look at a little too long. It may be any number of sexual temptations. But most men will admit to these sexual instincts and confess that at times they are almost uncontrollable. Most men confess that even when they try everything within their power to battle their unwanted urges, their animalistic instincts just can't be beaten.

The truth is that human sexuality is worlds apart from the animal instincts of the birds and bees. The difference? It's found in the most important sexual organ we humans have: our brains. The human sexual drive operates out of the cortex, that thin outer layer of the brain where all learning takes place. We use our highly developed brains to learn how, when, where, and whether they will give expression to our sexual urges — that's what separates us from the animals. In other words, because we are human we are responsible for our sexuality. We have the power — even when our biochemistry battles our brain — to make choices. We are more than our hormones. Unlike an animal's brain, our cortex allows us to control our urges.

The most telling difference between human and animal sexuality is this: all other animals perform sexual acts in the open, without embarrassment. Only human beings see any advantage to privacy. "Man is the only animal that blushes, or needs to," said Mark Twain. For us, sex is different. It has an aura of mystery about it, and instinctively we want to keep it separate, to experience it in private. We treat it as we treat religion, with an aura of apartness, or "holiness."

> *The happiness of a man in this life does not consist in the absence but in the mastery of his passions.*
>
> **Alfred, Lord Tennyson**

Still not convinced of our power to control sexual urges? Consider a male gynecologist who can clinically examine female sexual organs all day long without any sexual reaction and yet get aroused when he goes home and sees his wife in her nightgown. The reason? Brainpower.

In spite of this powerful means to managing our sexual urges, some men are convinced that their "animal instincts" are beyond their control — that the male sex drive is just too powerful to always manage. That's why

I dedicate this chapter to giving you proven methods for controlling your sex drive before it controls you.

The Dangerous Effects of Buying into This Myth

Before we jump into the specific methods for curbing your sexual instincts, I want to underscore both the deadly power of buying into the common misnomer that says your consuming sex drive is beyond your control and the powerful reward for learning to harness your raging hormones.

The idea that men think about sex every seven seconds (like the claim that we humans only use 10 percent of our brains) is often repeated but rarely sourced. Why? Because the number doesn't bear up against scrutiny. According to the *Kinsey Report* (*Sexual Behavior in the Human Male*), 54 percent of men think about sex every day or several times a day, 43 percent a few times a week or a few times a month, and 4 percent less than once a month. Even though the *Kinsey Report* relies on men to self-report how often they think about sex, it's still eye-opening to find that just under half of men aren't even thinking about sex once a day. Clearly, the seven-second rule may be a tad hyperbolic.

All this is not to diminish the human sex drive. It is admittedly powerful — right from the beginning. A little boy has his first erection within minutes after birth, and a little girl has her first vaginal lubrication within hours after birth. We are sexual beings. There's no denying it.

Sexuality is an integral part of who we are. It's how God made us. Even as a single person, there is no way you cannot be sexual. But I'll say it again: just because you are sexual does not mean you are doomed to be the victim of your raging hormones. Just because you are sexual doesn't mean you have to fall prey to the animal instinct of "doing it."

Let's assume that you've been married for ten years to a woman you met in college. The two of you love each other and are committed to spending the rest of your lives together. Periodically, though, your sexual needs are stronger than you are able to express and satisfy in your marriage. Sex is on your mind a lot, and your fantasies seem unrelenting. Sometimes you feel like you can hardly control your urges.

> *Living for his own pleasure is the least pleasurable thing a man can do; if his neighbors don't kill him in disgust, he will die slowly of boredom and lovelessness.*
>
> **Joy Davidman**

Now let's say a work colleague – a bright, pretty, divorced woman that you find attractive – suddenly begins showing up at your desk "just to chat." Before long, you notice how she stands closer to you than she needs to and she happens to arrive at the coffee machine at the same time you do. When she suggests you meet over dinner to discuss an upcoming presentation, her intentions are unmistakable.

What do you do? You don't give in, right? You're an honorable man who loves his wife. But do you turn down the woman's suggestion and still obsess that evening about what might have happened? Do you become aroused thinking of her? If so, you know you're playing with fire, right? But you say to yourself, *I can't help it — God made me this way.*

Indeed he did. But he also made you with a brain that allows you to stay alert, even when your hormones are running wild. He empowered you to stay in the driver's seat of your desires. He gives you an opportunity to choose how you'll use your powerful sex drive.

In this dilemma, and countless others, the last thing you want to do is to let your sexual impulses control you. They will press you to seek *immediate* gratification as they try to convince you to forget about any obvious repercussions. If you give in to your animalis-

> Men wake up aroused in the morning. We can't help it. We just wake up and we want you. And the women are thinking, "How can he want me the way I look in the morning?" It's because we can't see you. We have no blood anywhere near our optic nerve.
>
> **Andy Rooney**

tic instincts, you will inevitably endanger your marriage, undermine your values, and trade away long-term happiness for short-term satisfaction. Yet a staggering number of men have bought into the myth that they don't have a choice, and have done just that.

To put it bluntly, if your sexual impulses control you, your life will become a living hell. I've seen it countless times in my counseling practice. In their natural state, sexual urges are undisciplined, frighteningly unpredictable, and arrogantly demanding. That's why I want to provide you with the tools you need to rein in your impulses whenever they're about to get you into trouble.

Taming Your Animal Urges

Sexual feelings are a natural part of our biological inheritance. There is absolutely nothing wrong with these feelings. Sacred writings such as the Song of Songs celebrate the pure and sensuous love of a man and a woman. Sexual urges motivate us to engage in all sorts of constructive behaviors, produce a wide range of creative responses, and focus our attention on a person with whom we can form a long-term, meaningful marriage.

The trouble begins when these urges are not harnessed and managed within the bounds for which they were created. The following are a few of the time-tested techniques for putting healthy boundaries in place and maintaining them.

Check Your Sexual Speedometer

When I asked my friend Cliff Penner, who is also a psychologist and renowned Christian sex therapist, about the male myth that says our libidos are uncontrollable, he quickly told me the reason for its persistence. "If zero is 'no arousal' and ten is an orgasm," Cliff said, "men who reach an eight in their sexual arousal will find they've reached the point of no return."

He went on to describe the technical aspects of "ejaculatory inevitability." He stated that it was a physiological fact. Once a man reaches this stage, sexual release is unavoidable. You can't dial down your sex drive once it reaches that point. "That's why it feels to men as if they have no control over their sexual instincts," Cliff said, "when, of course, they do." The key is recognizing that the control diminishes the more you move in the direction of ejaculation.

It's like driving a car. You have far better control at a moderate speed, but once you reach racing speed the car becomes unmanageable. In this same regard, when you step on the sexual gas pedal of your libido you will reach a point where you become out of control.

"I can't help myself," is the common refrain from men who buy into this common myth. But that's only true if you reach the point in your sexual excitement scale where you physiologically can't turn back. Truth is, you have a significant amount of turnaround time even during full-on sexual excitement with an erect penis.

In fact, erections are emotionally tenuous. An erection can be stopped very easily when some nonsexual event occurs. For example, a sharp critical comment can make the erection diminish. So can the ringing of a cell phone or the knock on a door.

The point is that you have far more control over your sexual urges than you think you do — as long as you keep your sexual speedometer in check.

Recognize Your Rituals

"For me it starts around ten in the evening," Ron told me. "My wife typically goes to bed before I do and that's when the light from my computer screen seems to call out to me. I'll begin doing some work, checking email, and then 'innocently' searching for something online that I know will lead to some graphic images."

Ron was recounting his pre-arousal routine in a counseling session. "Once I spy something I know involves free porn, I click around for a few minutes ... but sometimes longer ... I'll sometimes look at the clock and realize I'm up past midnight still looking at images I convince myself that I never 'intended' to look at."

Ron was torn up inside. He'd carried out this little

ritual off and on for months on end before he came to see me. Ron didn't see himself as a sex addict. He wasn't scheduling his day around it. He wasn't seeking an affair or sex with a prostitute. But Ron was sexually frustrated. Sex with his wife wasn't all he wanted it to be and that was part of his justification for his "innocent" surfing sessions on his computer. And this too-frequent ritual was adding to his "uncontrollable" libido.

> *The instinct of fidelity is perhaps the deepest instinct in the great complex we call sex. Where there is real sex there is the underlying passion for fidelity.*
>
> **D. H. Lawrence**

If you want to find freedom from an uninhibited sex drive, like Ron, you've got to identify the rituals that precede an episode of acting out. Rituals men have mentioned to me include surfing the Internet, driving by a strip club, reading personal ads, browsing in a video store, calling a former girlfriend, TV channel surfing, cruising in a red-light district, calling 900-numbers just for information, and asking a female acquaintance out to lunch.

To break out of the trap, make a list of the rituals that lead up to destructive sexual behavior for you. Then name the aggressive steps you'll take to contain each ritual. Expect your lustful nature to resist, to plead with you to keep your favorite ritual. You must ignore its pleadings and ruthlessly do whatever it takes. Holding on to even one ritual will nurture the unhealthy side of your libido.

I know a man who removed cable TV from his home. As a further precaution, he refused to watch TV after ten o'clock in the evening unless his wife was present. I know another man who refuses to turn on the TV in his hotel room if he's traveling alone. By never turning it on, he avoids the ritual of channel surfing. For other men, it may mean signing up with an online server that blocks access to pornographic sites on the web.

You get the idea. If you want to better control your animal urges, you'll need to be aware of the rituals you go through to get sexually stimulated. Every man is different in this regard, but you know what you do to get your kicks.

Try a Counter Image

One of the most common refrains I hear from men in my counseling office – men who are trying to better manage their libido – is that it only takes one innocent glance toward a woman in a tight sweater or a short skirt, for example, and their sexual stallions are off to the races. Their mind begins to whirl with excitement. "I don't have any control over it," they say. "It's like a switch that flips, and all I can think about is sex until I get some relief."

Truth be told, it *is* like a switch that gets flipped. A subtle but sensual image can trigger a cascade of biochemicals in your body and start the physiological process of getting sexually turned on – if you let it. You see, it's a switch that you can control. You have the power to turn it on and turn it off. And the switch is located in your mind.

You won't find a psychologist on the planet who doesn't agree with this. Your thoughts control your sexual excitement, and you can control your thoughts. You can choose to either feed or starve your sexual thoughts. It's completely within your control.

You've heard it said that you can "choose to be happy." Well, you can also choose to be sexually excited – or not. How? Let's say you've inadvertently caught a glimpse through a peek-a-boo blouse that triggers your mind into a sexual excitement that is on the verge of a full-blown fantasy. If you want to stop it before it even happens, you simply need to focus your attention on anything else.

Now, I know that image may be pulling you toward it like a magnet – you may feel helpless in your efforts to resist it – but your mind is more powerful than you think. I can't tell you what counter thought is going to work best for you, but I promise that you have one. And if you find it, it will defeat the sequence of sexual thoughts attempting to control you. For example, it may be a thought about your wife and kids. It may be imagining what your father or your pastor might say in the situation. It may be a Bible verse such as, "Walk in the Spirit, and you shall not fulfill the lust of the flesh" (Galatians 5:16). It may be replaying a favorite sports experience. It may be the thought of sailing or some other hobby.

The point is that you can only extinguish an unwanted thought by *replacing* it with another thought. Simply saying something like, "I shouldn't think about this" won't work. You've got to deliberately put a new thought in its place — or better yet, put your wife into the picture.

Author and pastor John Piper likens this process to a war in the mind. He says, "We must not give a sexual image or impulse more than five seconds before we mount a violent counterattack with the mind." He calls them lust-destroying images and urges men to find an image that is "so powerful that the other image cannot survive."[1]

Never fall for the false belief that you are helpless against your unwanted sexual thoughts. Your mind is more powerful than you think, and you are sitting at the controls.

Free Your Mind

It should almost go without saying, but not quite: If you want to better manage your libido, you've got to monitor what you're putting in your mind. You've heard this before, I know, but it bears a quick underscoring.

Consider something as simple as music. In an eye-opening study, researchers found that teenagers who listen to lyrics filled with sexual innuendos and explicit sex talk are more likely to indulge in early sexual activity than their counterparts who don't.

In 2001, the researchers surveyed 1,461 teenagers between the ages of 12 and 17. Most of the participants were virgins at the beginning of the study. Between 2002 and 2004, the researchers carried out follow-up interviews to track the sexual developments in the teens' lives. Around 51 percent of teens whose music collection consisted of sexually degrading music began having sex within two years of the three-year study as opposed to 29 percent of those who did not listen to such music.[2]

Sex is just about the most powerful and explosive force that is built into us. Every instinct and every bit of counseling experience I have had tells me it is too dangerous a commodity to be handed over to people with no strings attached.

Norman Vincent Peale

Now, maybe you think you're not as impressionable as the teenagers in this study. But that's doubtful. A mountain of research reveals that what we feed our brain, at any age, plays a significant role, not just in what we think, but what we do. Whether it's movies, television, or websites, they all shape our behavior, even as adults. You may want to say, "It's just a movie." I understand. But just so you know, almost every teenager in this study said at the outset, "It's just music."

I'll say it again. What we feed our minds, what we expose ourselves to — whatever our age — influences what we do. So if you are feeding your brain something that is contributing to an overpowering libido, consider how a change in this habit just might free your mind and empower you with more control over your sexual urges.

Consider Confiding — Carefully

Because I'm a professor on a Christian college campus, I'm sometimes invited into a residence hall to speak to a group of men who live on the same floor. More often than not, they ask me to address some aspect of sexuality and relationships. And nearly every time I do this, some of the guys, one by one in the days that follow, will show up at my office and confess some sexual behavior they are ashamed of. They'll often tell me that they haven't told anyone else. After I've listened with compassion and maybe prayed with them, asking God for a new start, they will inevitably say, "It feels so good to finally tell somebody about this."

> *Saving grace makes a man as willing to leave his lusts as a slave is willing to leave his galley, or a prisoner his dungeon, or a thief his bolts, or a beggar his rags.*
>
> **Thomas Brooks**

Confession is good for the soul. It's true. But confession isn't the point. *A change in behavior following a confession* is the goal. That's why, whenever one of these young men seeks me out following a talk I've given, I tell them that I'm happy to hear their story as long as they realize that confession isn't enough to change their behavior—it's just a start.

Maybe that's a start you need. If your unwieldy libido is getting you to do things you don't want to do, confessing the scenario can be a great catalyst for progress. But this needs to be done carefully. It needs to be done with the right person at the right time. I can't tell you who that is for you, but chances are it's either a good friend you respect and trust, or maybe a counselor or minister. In some cases, it could even be your wife. But, like I said, it has to be done carefully.

My friend Gary Thomas, author of *Authentic Faith*, is quicker to encourage this than I am. He recounts the story of a young seminarian married just a few years, who shared with him his lapse into pornography. He'd developed a habit before marriage, but early on in his marriage he'd avoided it. After a couple of years, however, he again gave in and eventually shared his lapse with his wife.

> *"Thou shalt not commit adultery." This sizzling sentence is not intended to take the joy out of our sex lives, but to put more pride and pleasure into our sexual activity by protecting us, first of all, from shame and low self-esteem than from alienation, bitterness, cynicism, fear, and finally — loneliness!*
>
> **Robert Schuller**

The result of his confession to his wife? She had horror on her face. She felt betrayed and hurt. "When I think about pornography," he said, "I think about how much I hurt my wife. I don't want to repeat that." In other words, this man conditioned his mind to associate pornography with pain, not pleasure.

If you feel that confession of something like this to your wife would be helpful, I would urge you to get some professional coaching in the process. I've also seen a scenario like this backfire. If you're considering it, know that it needs to be done prayerfully and carefully.

Do the Unnatural

Many men indulge their sexual urges and justify unhealthy sexual behaviors by calling these sexual inclinations "natural." They say this as if anything that is "natural" means that you have license to do it. "It's part of my nature," they say. But there's a major flaw in this thinking.

Calling something natural does not mean it is inevitable, essential, beneficial, or inflexible. As psychiatrist M. Scott Peck pointed out years ago, "It

> *Each of you should learn to control his own body in a way that is holy and honorable.*
>
> **1 Thessalonians 4:4**

is also natural to defecate in our pants and never brush our teeth. Yet we teach ourselves to do the unnatural until the unnatural itself becomes second nature. Indeed, all self-discipline might be defined as teaching ourselves to do the unnatural."[3]

Did you catch that? Doing the unnatural is the result of self-discipline. "He who ignores discipline," says Proverbs 15:32, "despises himself." In other words, without self-discipline, without delaying our gratification, we end up void of dignity. We lose our self-respect. In fact, Jewish theologian and philosopher Abraham J. Heschel says, "Self-respect is the fruit of discipline; the sense of dignity grows with the ability to say no to oneself."

And that's exactly what it takes to curb your unbridled libido. It requires you to say no to yourself. Unnatural? Maybe. But it is the sure path to managing your animal instincts, and it brings with it the fruit of dignity.

Is There Really Such a Thing As a "Sex Addict"?

Before we leave this chapter, I feel compelled to address the issue of sexual addiction. The term "sexual addiction" was coined a few years back by Dr. Patrick Carnes to describe people with an obsessive sex drive. This is different than a normal libido that sometimes seems unmanageable. The person with a bona fide sex addiction is suffering significant consequences as a result of not being able to stop anything from Internet sex to obsessive masturbation to affairs.

Much like the person addicted to drugs, alcohol, or gambling, the sex addict has an insatiable need that constantly nags at them. And their need is actually not for sex; it is really about pain, or more accurately, escaping emotional pain or anxiety.

So they dull the pain with obsessive sex. It becomes their drug. Sex addicts may feel deeply ashamed because of it. They may ruin relationships because of it. They may contract diseases because of it. They may lose lots of money because of it. But no matter how many times they try to stop, they can't.

> *Our passions are like convulsion fits, which, though they make us stronger for the time, leave us the weaker ever after.*
>
> **Johnathan Swift**

So why can't people just stop these behaviors? If there's no drug or chemical involved, how is sex addiction like drug addiction or smoking? "When you have a compulsive gambler," says Carnes, "you're not taking a chemical.... In other words, we produce chemicals in our brain whether we use an outside chemical or not."[4] That's precisely why this is an "addiction."

By the way, no diagnosis for sexual addiction is described in the pages of the *Diagnostic and Statistical Manual of Mental Disorders*, or *DSM*. Psychologists use the definitions in the *DSM* as a means of diagnosing—and treating—mental health problems. But that doesn't jibe with the experience of many mental health professionals, who see people coming into their offices displaying symptoms of out-of-control sexual desire.

If you feel that you may be contending with more than a powerful libido, if your sex drive is truly out of control, I urge you to seek professional help.

There are several recovery programs that can be checked out online. For places to begin, see the list on pages 194–95 of this book.

One more thing. I want you to know that if you are feeling controlled by a sexual addiction, you can—without a doubt—get control over it. I've seen it countless times. You don't have to live with this overwhelming drive that repeatedly gets you into trouble. With the help I've outlined in this chapter, you can live a life free from this unhealthy compulsion. You can live like a new man, in full control of your own urges. The resources for moving past this are waiting for you. It all begins with making the decision to get the help you need.

For Reflection

1. On a scale of one to ten, where would you rate your personal control over your libido and why?

2. What was the single most helpful piece of information you gleaned from this chapter and why?

3. When are you least in control of your libido and what is one practical thing you can do in that situation to manage it more effectively?

 Check this out! You'll find a special online video feature specifically designed to augment what you have just read in this chapter, along with a message from Dr. Parrott. Go to CrazyGoodSex.jLog.com/Ch6 to find the jLog for Myth 6.

A Note to the Curious Woman about Sex Drive

I can almost hear some women reading this chapter and saying, "C'mon! You've got to be kidding me! No control over your sexual urges?" I understand. Trust me, I've counseled enough couples where the husband seemed to give into every urge conceivable and the wife was left wondering what kind of animal she married. You may be thinking that some men are just looking for an excuse to justify their stupid sexual decisions. And I'd have to agree with you. Every man, no matter how powerful his libido, is ultimately responsible for how much he gives in to its power.

As a wife of a man who may sometimes feel like his sex drive is more powerful than he is, however, you may want to consider ways that you can help him keep it under consistent control. I'm not talking about you having to be the one responsible for his decisions in this area. Not at all. I want to make this clear: He is ultimately responsible. But as "iron sharpens iron" you can help him in this effort.

You can begin by exploring his sex drive with him. I've facilitated this conversation several times with couples in counseling, and the best place to start is by asking him when he, generally speaking, is most likely to feel the weakest control over his urges. What you'll discover is that he feels most vulnerable to his sex drive when he is stressed out or exhausted. Most men make their worst decisions when they are tired, feeling beat down, and not appreciated. The same is true for you, too, by the way.

So, you don't have to be a psychologist to figure out what you can do to keep him on the straight and narrow when he's feeling down and out. Tune into his sexual needs when he's tired, stressed, and fatigued.

Crazy Good Sex
with Your Wife

There is nothing wrong with making love with the light on. Just make sure the car door is closed.

George Burns

A modern Orthodox Jewish couple, preparing for a religious wedding, meets with their rabbi for counseling. The rabbi asks if they have any last questions before they leave.

The man asks, "Rabbi, we realize it's tradition for men to dance with men, and women to dance with women at the reception. But we'd like your permission to dance together, like the rest of the world."

"Absolutely not," says the rabbi. "It's immodest. Men and women always dance separately."

"So after the ceremony, I can't even dance with my own wife?"

"No," answered the rabbi. "It's forbidden."

"Well, okay," says the man, "What about sex? Can we finally have sex?"

"Of course!" replies the rabbi. "Sex is a mitzvah — a good thing within marriage, to have children!"

"What about different positions?" asks the man.

"No problem," says the rabbi. "It's a mitzvah!"

"Woman on top?" the man asks.

"Sure," says the rabbi. "Go for it! It's a mitzvah!"

"Doggy style?"

"Sure! Another mitzvah!"

"On the kitchen table?"

"Yes, yes! A mitzvah!"

"Can we do it on rubber sheets with a bottle of hot oil, a leather harness, and a bucket of honey?"

"You may indeed. It's all a mitzvah!"

"Can we do it standing up?"

"No." says the rabbi."

"Why not?" asks the man.

"Could lead to dancing."

I began this book by saying there's a lot of crazy thinking about sex. And this silly joke speaks for itself. The point of my book, of course, is not to simply highlight the biggest myths men have about sex. It's to shed light on them in the hopes that you would ultimately enjoy crazy good sex with your wife.

That's my prayer for you. That you would never separate sex from the sacred. That your sex life would be everything God intended it to be. That it would be crazy good — but never stupid.

I hope you'll join me online at RealRelationships.com with questions and comments to further explore this vitally important topic.

Helpful Organizations and Resources

*Identifies an organization or resource that focuses specifically on sexual addiction

- **Bethesda Workshop with Marnie Ferree***
  Nashville, Tennessee
  bethesdaworkshops.org

- **Celebrate Recovery®***
  celebraterecovery.com

- **Co-Dependents Anonymous***
  coda.org

- **Faithful & True Ministries***
  Eden Prairie, Minnesota
  faithfulandtrueministries.com

- **Heart to Heart Counseling Center***
  Colorado Springs, Colorado
  sexaddict.com

- **L.I.F.E. Ministries***
  freedomeveryday.org

- **New Life Ministries**
  Laguna Beach, California
  everymansbattle.com

- **Operation Integrity***
  Monarch Beach, California
  operationintegrity.org

- **Overcomers Outreach***
  overcomersoutreach.org

- **Passionate Commitment***
  passionatecommitment.com

- **Prodigals International**
  Kirkland, Washington
  prodigalsonline.org

- **Pure Desire Ministries International**
  Gresham, Oregon
  puredesire.org

- **Pure Warrior Ministries**
  Valleyford, Washington
  purewarrior.org

- **Samson Society***
  samsonsociety.org

Notes

Kinky and Corny: The Honest Reason I Wrote This Book

[1] John Mooney, *The Destroying Angel: Sex, Fitness and Food in the Legacy of Degeneracy Theory, Graham Crackers, Kellogg's Corn Flakes and American Healthy History* (Buffalo: Prometheus Books, 1985).

[2] *U.S. Census Bureau. www.census.gov/Press-Release/www/releases/archives/marital_status_living_arrangements/000500.html.*

What Hugh Hefner Never Figured Out

[1] *Politically Incorrect*, ABC Television (2-15-01).

[2] Brian Murra, "Bare Nekkid Ladies: Hugh Hefner and the mainstreaming of pornography." *The Weekly Standard*, Volume 9, August 2, 2004, 44.

[3] *Newsweek* cover, August 4, 1986.

[4] Matthew Scully, "The Playboy Legacy," *Wall Street Journal*, March 31, 2006.

[5] Ibid.

[6] If you are a student of church history, you know that there was a period dating back to St. Augustine, where Christians strayed from Scripture and portrayed sex to be sinful. Church fathers created a restrictive, legalistic sexual economy, robbing couples of the ability to enjoy God's intended pleasure.

[7] This phrase, "the gift of sex," originated with Cliff and Joyce Penner.

[8] Philip Yancey, *Rumors of Another World* (Grand Rapids: Zondervan, 2003).

Myth 1: Men Want More Sex Than Women Do

[1] "Standard Deviation," *Everybody Loves Raymond*, Season 1, Disc 1 (New York: HBO Home Video, 2004).

[2] Daniel G. Amen, *Sex on the Brain* (New York: Random House, 2007).

[3] Anita H. Clayton, "Women's mental health." *Psychiatric Clinics of North America*, 26 (3), (2003): 132–48.

[4] J. Brines, "Economic dependency, gender and the division of labor at home." *The American Journal of Sociology*, 199 (3), (1994): 652–88.

[5] See also, D. M. Buss and T. K. Shackelford. "A half century of mate preferences: the cultural evolution of values." *Journal of Marriage and Family*, 63 (2), (2001): 491–503.

Myth 2: Sex with the Same Person Gets Boring

[1] Robert T. Michael, et. al., "Sex in America: A Definitive Survey." *New England Journal of Medicine*, http://content.nejm.org/cgi/content/extract/332/21/1452.

[2] "Sex: Myths, Lies and Straight Talk," *20/20*, ABC Television. November 5, 2004.

[3] Linda J. Waite and Maggie Gallagher, *The Case for Marriage* (New York: Broadway, 2000), 155.

[4] A 1994 study by the National Opinion Research center at the University of Chicago found that married couples in America generally enjoy more frequent and satisfying sexual activity than singles. Yet when married couples in America go to the movie theater or rent a video to catch Hollywood's latest hit, they're not likely to see couples on screen that are similar to them.

[5] William R. Mattox Jr., "The Hottest Valentines." The *Washington*

Post, 1994. The survey was commissioned by the Family Research Council. Data was collected from a nationwide random telephone sample of 1,100 people, conducted by an independent Bethesda firm, and analyzed by an American University psychologist.

[6] Michael, R. T., Gagnon, J. H. and Lauman, E. O. (1994). Sex in American: A Definitive Survey, Boston: Little, Brown & Co., p. 124.

[7] Michael et al, p. 125.

[8] L. H. Bukstel, et. al., "Projected extramarital sexual involvement in unmarried college students." *Journal of Marriage and the Family,* 40 (1978): 337–40.

[9] William R. Mattox Jr., "The Hottest Valentines."

[10] Clarence Page, "Remembering the Big Dipper's Other Statistics," *Chicago Tribune,* October 17, 1999.

[11] Kathleen Deveny, "We're not in the Mood." *Newsweek,* June 30, 2003, 43.

[12] Tom W. Smith, "American Sexual Behavior: Trend, Socio-Demographic Differences, and Risk Behavior," *National Opinion Research Center,* University of Chicago, GSS Topical Report No. 25, March 2006.

[13] Margaret Carlson, "The Mummy Diaries." *Time,* October 7, 2002.

Myth 3: Porn Is Not Addictive

[1] Top Ten Reviews, "Internet Pornography Statistics," http://internet-filter-review.toptenreviews.com/internet-pornography-statistics.html.

[2] Research indicates that some kind of connection does exist. Important studies have been undertaken by leading experts in North America, including Dr. Dolf Zillmann at Indiana University, Dr. Jennings Bryant at the University of Houston, James Weaver at the University of Kentucky, Dr. Edward Donnerstein at the University of Wisconsin, Dr. Neil Malamuth at UCLA,

and Dr. James Check at York University in Canada. The conclusions drawn from their research do not demonstrate an airtight cause-and-effect relationship between pornography and sexual violence; however, this is due to the simple reason that it is nearly impossible to conclusively prove cause and effect in any social science research. But the evidence gathered is enough to say that there seems to be a very real correlation between the two.

[3] "Only in America," *The Week*, (March 17, 2006).

[4] Mind Hacks, "Attack of the Porno Zombies." http://www.mindhacks.com/blog/2005/07/attack_of_the_porno.html.

[5] Ryan Singel, "Internet Porn: Worse than Crack?" *Wired*, November 19, 2004, www.wired.com/science/discoveries/news/2004/11/65772.

[6] T. C. Morgan, "Porn's Stranglehold." *Christianity Today*, March 2008, 7.

[7] Ibid., 30.

[8] Al Cooper, "Study: 200,000 Hooked on Web Porn," *Journal of Sexual Addiction and Compulsivity*, as seen on Salon.com, March 1, 2000.

[9] Victor B. Cline, "Pornography's Effects on Adults & Children," (New York: Morality in Media, 1999), 5.

[10] Pamela Paul, "The Porn Factor." *Time*, January 19, 2004.

Myth 4: Size Matters

[1] Conversation with Cliff and Joyce Penner.

[2] A. Fathy, et. al., "Experiences with Promedon Malleable Penile Implant." *Urology*, 79(3), (2007): 244–47.

Myth 5: The Bible Is Very Clear on Masturbation

[1] Mark Driscoll, "Masturbation and Lust," YouTube. www.youtube.com/results?search_query=mark+driscoll+masturbation&search_type=&aq=0.

[2] R. Crooks and K. Baur, *Our Sexuality* (4th ed.), (New York: Benjamin/Cummings, 1990).

[3] G. Wood and E. Ruddock, *Vitalogy* (Chicago: Vitalogy Association, 1918).

[4] *TrueChristian*, www.TrueChristian.com.

[5] J. D. Atwood and J. Gagnon, "Masturbatory behavior in college youth." *Journal of Sex Education and Therapy*, 13 (2), (1987): 35–42.

[6] A. Hart, *The Sexual Man: Masculinity without Guilt* (Dallas: Word, 1994).

[7] S. S. and C. L. Janus, *The Janus Report on Sexual Behavior* (New York: Wiley and Sons, 1993), 31.

[8] Two passages that are most often used to condemn masturbation are Genesis 38:8–10 and 1 Corinthians 6:9–10. However, most scholars examining these passages do not see them addressing the issue of masturbation.

[9] R. E. Butman, "Masturbation." *Baker Encyclopedia of Psychology* (Grand Rapids: Baker, 1985).

[10] R. J. Foster, *Money, Sex & Power* (San Francisco: Harper & Row, 1985).

[11] Consider the variety of positions on this issue taken by Christians: Stephen Grunlan, in his book, *Marriage and the Family: A Christian Perspective* (Zondervan, 1984), gives three reasons why Christians should avoid masturbation: First, there is no biological necessity for masturbation; second, masturbation is a solo act, and God created humans as sexual beings to bring men and women together; third, the fantasies and thought life that accompany the act. On the other hand, James Dobson, in his popular "Focus on the Family" film series, accepts masturbation as a normal part of growing up unless it becomes excessive. Charlie Shedd, in *The Stork Is Dead* (Word, 1976), speaks of it as a "gift from God." David Semands (in J. A. Petersen's *For Families Only*, Tyndale, 1977), says "It's high time we stop making such a big

deal of masturbation and give it the well-deserved unimportance it merits."

[12]Zondervan, 1984.

[13]Daniel Heimbach, *True Sexual Morality* (Wheaton, Ill.: Crossway, 2004).

[14]Word, 1976.

[15]Douglas Rosenau, *A Celebration of Sex* (Nashville: Thomas Nelson, 2002).

[16]Word, 1994.

[17]J. A. Petersen, *For Families Only* (Wheaton, Ill.: Tyndale, 1977).

[18]Frederick Buechner, *Wishful Thinking: A Theological ABC* (San Francisco: HarperSanFrancisco, 1973), 65.

[19]W. R. Johnson, *Masturbation* (New York: Sex Information and Education Council of the U.S.).

[20]M. A. May, *A Christian Guide to Sexual Counseling* (Grand Rapids: Zondervan, 1987), 193.

[21]Stephen Grunlan, *Marriage and the Family: A Christian Perspective* (Grand Rapids: Zondervan, 1984), 122.

[22]Steve Gerali, *The Struggle* (Colorado Springs: NavPress, 2003), 133.

Myth 6: My Sex Drive Is Too Powerful to Control

[1]John Piper, from the sermon "A Passion for Purity versus Passive Prayers," www.desiringGod.org (11–10–99).

[2]Sunil Vyas, "Raunchy Lyrics Trigger Earlier Onset of Sexual Activity among Teens," *Pediatrics* (2006).

[3]M. Scott Peck, *The Road Less Traveled* (New York: Touchstone, 1998).

[4]Patrick Carnes, *Clinical Management of Sex Addiction* (New York: Brunner-Toutledge, 2002).

Les Parrott is founder of the Center for Relationship Development on the campus of Seattle Pacific University and the bestselling author of *High-Maintenance Relationships*, *The Control Freak*, and *Love Talk*. Dr. Parrott is a sought-after speaker to Fortune 500 companies and holds relationship seminars across North America. He also hosts the national radio broadcast *Love Talk*. Dr. Parrott has been featured in *USA Today*, the *Wall Street Journal*, and the *New York Times*. His television appearances include CNN, *Good Morning America*, and *Oprah*.

www.RealRelationships.com

Join me and others on an exciting journey with *Crazy Good Sex* at my online Journey Log™ – or jLog™ for short.

The *Crazy Good Sex* jLog™ is designed with you in mind. It'll take you through an interactive video experience that allows you to engage more deeply with the book, with other readers, and with me. I think you'll enjoy it. Join the journey with me right now at <u>crazygoodsex.jlog.com</u>

Dr. Les Parrott

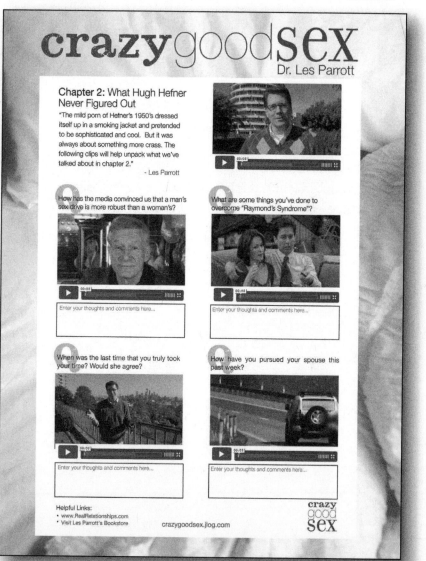

crazygoodsex
Dr. Les Parrott

Chapter 2: What Hugh Hefner Never Figured Out

"The mild porn of Hefner's 1950's dressed itself up in a smoking jacket and pretended to be sophisticated and cool. But it was always about something more crass. The following clips will help unpack what we've talked about in chapter 2."

- Les Parrott

How has the media convinced us that a man's sex drive is more robust than a woman's?

Enter your thoughts and comments here...

What are some things you've done to overcome "Raymond's Syndrome"?

Enter your thoughts and comments here...

When was the last time that you truly took your time? Would she agree?

Enter your thoughts and comments here...

How have you pursued your spouse this past week?

Enter your thoughts and comments here...

Helpful Links:
• www.RealRelationships.com
• Visit Les Parrott's Bookstore

crazygoodsex.jlog.com

crazy good sex

In our efforts to help couples build strong, lifelong marriages, we have pioneered a growing movement called Marriage Mentoring — where a seasoned and experienced couple is linked with a less experienced couple. We offer this brief synopsis to readers who are interested in learning more about this effort and how they can become part of it.

The Sleeping Giant
of Marriage Mentoring

Drs. Les and Leslie Parrott

In his book *Did You Spot the Gorilla?* psychologist Richard Wiseman describes an experiment where volunteers watched a thirty-second video of two teams playing basketball and were asked to count the number of times one of the teams passed the ball. What they weren't told was that halfway through the video, a man dressed in a gorilla suit would run onto the court, stand in front of the camera, and beat his chest. Amazingly only a few of the volunteers spotted the man in the gorilla suit. Most of the volunteers were so intent on counting passes that they completely missed the gorilla.

Wiseman concluded that most people go through life so focused on the task at hand they completely miss what would otherwise be obvious. Has the church fallen victim to this same phenomenon? Are we blind to the gorilla of marriage mentoring? After all, it's a slumbering giant visible in every congregation—a team of couples who have what it takes to make a powerful impact on marriages around them. And yet, for the most part, they haven't been tapped. They've been neglected or unrecognized.

We intend to change all that. We want to awaken the sleeping giant of marriage mentors in the local church and enable them to seize an opportunity that has been too long neglected.

Would It Make a Difference?

Whether you know it or not, some people in your congregation may not look particularly needy or desperate for help, but many of them are. Countless couples, on any given weekend, file into churches across the country, looking their "Sunday best," and quietly keeping a marriage problem to themselves. The stigma of counseling may be keeping them from seeking help. Or they may feel all alone, that nobody else would understand. Or they may simply have nobody to talk to. But truth be told, some of these couples are going down. Their marriages are hurting and nobody has recognized their signal for help—and even if they have, they don't feel it's their place to step in.

Surely you've witnessed a painful divorce where trouble was never suspected. You've certainly seen the newly-wed couple, full of promise, whose marriage is short-lived because they didn't get a solid start. And think of the numerous couples in your care who are stuck in a rut, not reaching their full potential.

Now, think of the difference it would make if these couples in your congregation could be linked with other couples, more seasoned and experienced in what these couples are going through. Would it make any difference? You bet. How do we know? Because we've been recruiting, screening, and training couples to become marriage mentors for more than a decade. We've heard their stories. We've done the research. Marriage mentoring works.

Consider the facts. There are close to 400,000 churches in America.* If just one-third of these churches would recruit and train ten mentor couples each, that would mean one million marriage mentors. Think of the difference that would make! With a mighty band of marriage mentors we could surely save half of the 1.2 million marriages that end in divorce each year. And think of the marriages that could move from good to great if only they had another couple with more experience to walk beside them.

Truth be told, they do. Every congregation, no matter how big or small, has the potential to awaken the marriage mentors in its midst. With far too many marriages suffering in silence and with far too many couples merely getting by, it's high time we, the church, do something. And we can.

---

*Cf. Thom S. Rainer, *Breakout Churches* (Grand Rapids: Zondervan, 2005), 13.

We Must Do Something

One morning, near the turn of the twentieth century, Bramwell Booth visited his elderly father, William Booth, founder of the Salvation Army.

"Bramwell, did you know that men slept out all night on the bridges?" William had arrived in London very late the night before from a town in the south of England and had to cross through the capital to reach his home. What he had seen on that midnight return accounted for his inquiry.

"Well, yes," Bramwell replied, "a lot of poor fellows, I suppose, do that."

"Then go and do something!" William said. "We must do something."

"What can we do?"

"Get them shelter."

"That will cost money."

"Something must be done. Get hold of a warehouse and warm it, and find something to cover them!"

That was the beginning of the Salvation Army shelters. And if William Booth was alive today he just might have the same passion for "doing something" about the sad state of marriage. And make no mistake about it, the state of marriage is sad.

We've all heard the startling statistics of divorce. Almost anyone can tell you that "half of all marriages end in divorce." We're almost immune to the numbers. It gets a little closer to home when you ask an average congregation to raise their hands if they have had someone in their family or a close friend suffer a divorce. Nearly every hand goes up. We all know something needs to be done, but for the most part we haven't known what to do. Or worse, we think very little or nothing can be done.

But by now, you know that we beg to differ with this stance. Something can be done. And something is already being done in many churches around North America. Let us tell you what we mean.

Our Story

Fifteen years ago we first began using the term *marriage mentors* in relationship to a program we developed called *Saving Your Marriage Before It Starts.* Through a seminar we launched in Seattle we were beginning to help hundreds of newlyweds get started on the right foot. But soon into our efforts we began to wonder whether the information we were teaching was actually sticking. We began to wonder how we could build in some accountability for these couples who went through our program, to be sure they were actually putting the information into practice.

There were too many for us to follow up on personally, so we began to recruit older, more experienced couples, to meet with these newlyweds. Without much training at first, we asked them to simply check in with their assigned couple every so often to see how things were going. And it didn't take us long to realize that something exciting was happening because of this fledgling notion. We were beginning to hear remarkable stories convincing us that the time-honored tool of mentoring is more than ready to be applied to marriage (NOTE: see sidebar: The Marriage Mentoring Triad).

Tom and Wendy, a typical newly married couple, were among the first to experience our program. In their mid-twenties, they had dated for nearly two years before getting engaged. They had the blessing of their parents, attended premarital counseling, and were on their way to living happily ever after—or so everyone thought.

But marriage for Tom and Wendy, like the majority of newlyweds, wasn't all they hoped for. Each of them, for different reasons, felt a bit slighted. Unlike the majority of couples, however, Tom and Wendy talked openly about their feelings. The expectations they had of marriage were not getting met and they were determined to do something about it. So on a cold January day, eight months after their wedding, Tom and Wendy asked for help.

The Guinea Pig Couple

Bundled up against the cold, they came into our office and began to shed their coats. As Wendy sipped hot coffee to thaw out, she said, "We have talked to friends and family about what is going on, but we both decided we needed more objectivity."

Tom joined in: "Yeah, everybody who knows us just says 'give it time' or something like that." Their marriage, he went on to say, was not suffering a major trauma; it didn't need an overhaul, just "a little realignment."

We met with Tom and Wendy for nearly an hour, listening to their experience. We gave them a couple of exercises to help them explore their misconceptions of marriage and we recommended a few resources. Then we talked about the idea of linking up with a marriage mentor couple.

"What's that?" they both asked.

We told them how meeting from time to time with a more seasoned married couple could give them a sounding board and a safe place to explore some of their questions about marriage. Like most newlyweds we talk to, Tom and Wendy were very eager to find such a couple. After a bit of discussion, they suggested a married couple in their church. Neither of them knew the couple very well, but they respected their marriage from afar and thought they would fit the bill. After a couple of phone calls and a little more exploration, we made the connection for Tom and Wendy. Over the course of several months, they met several times with their mentors, Nate and Sharon. Tom and Wendy found the marriage mentoring extremely helpful. Here is a portion of a letter they wrote to us back then:

Dear Les and Leslie,

How can we ever thank you for helping us find a marriage mentor couple? Before coming to you we had never even heard of such an idea. But needless to say, our mentoring relationship with Nate and Sharon ended up being the most important thing we have ever done to build up our marriage. It was so nice to have another couple know what we were going through and remain objective at the same time.

We have since moved to another state, but on our wedding anniversary, Nate and Sharon always give us a call to celebrate our marriage.

Anyway, we are writing to say thank you and to say that you should tell more people about the benefits of marriage mentoring. Someday we hope to give back the gift that Nate and Sharon gave to us by mentoring some newly married couples. We think every couple just starting out should have a mentor.

That's not a bad idea, we thought to ourselves. And we've made it standard practice ever since for every newlywed couple who has been part of our *Saving Your Marriage Before It Starts* program. We have literally linked thousands of newlyweds with mentors over the last decade.

How They're Doing Today

As we were writing this we began to get curious about Tom and Wendy, so we tracked them down. Now living in Portland, Oregon, Wendy and Tom have been married fifteen years and have two children. They are not the perfect couple, but they are madly in love and happier than they ever imagined. In an email we received from Wendy just this week, she revealed a "secret" to their success.

> *As one of the first couples in your group to go though the mentoring process we became quick converts. We immediately saw the advantage to having Nate and Sharon, a couple we didn't even know at the start, in our lives. They made a world of difference for us.*
>
> *And you might be pleased to know that we've followed up on our intentions to give back what they gave to us. A few years ago we began to do some mentoring ourselves. Our church didn't have a mentoring program and we thought it was time that they did—so we started one. We now have six other mentoring couples who work with us and we're having a blast. As Tom often says, "It's the best thing we do all year for our own marriage." He's right. Meeting with our mentorees brings us closer together and it feels so right to know we are doing some good ... just like Nate and Sharon did for us.*
>
> *By the way, they still send us an anniversary card every year!*

As you might imagine, this email was certainly encouraging. Because of Tom and Wendy, and thousands of couples we've met with just like them, we come to the enterprise of marriage mentoring with great conviction and passion. And with a vision for what might be.

The Dream

We have a dream that one day a massive network of marriage mentors will undergird the state of marriage across North America and around the world. Serving as a type of relational safety net, these mentors will lift up and support couples at crucial crossroads — those just starting out, about to have a baby, in crisis, raising teenagers, looking to maximize their marriage, whatever. Marriage mentoring applies to every stage and phase of married life.

It's a dream we've been talking about wherever we can. In fact, just a few years ago, the governor of Oklahoma invited us to move to his state (where they have one of the highest divorce rates in the country) for one year. And we did. Why? It gave us the opportunity to meet with hundreds of clergy and thousands of lay couples just to talk about our dream of marriage mentoring. We've also talked about it on national radio and television. We've spoken about it in dozens of conferences. We've written about it in numerous magazines and newspapers.

We've been preaching "marriage mentoring" for so long in so many places with so little repercussion that we sometimes wondered if anyone was listening. But no longer.

We are encouraged. Very encouraged. More than ever, we are seeing the church awaken to this idea and catch on to this dream. In fact, we now receive emails every day with requests for more information on marriage mentoring. If you google "marriage mentoring" your search will return over a half million webpages dealing with the idea in some fashion. More and more churches identify themselves as having a marriage mentoring ministry. And in a recent survey, 62 percent of respondents said they'd like to find a mentor couple in their church, and 92 percent said they would especially like to have a mentor to help them through times of conflict.*

The times are changing. We're hearing the rumblings of a sleeping giant about to wake up. And we're hoping you will prayerfully consider being a part of it.

---

*Shane Fookes, "Marriage and Family Mentoring," *Family Life* white paper (2004), 4.

What Is Marriage Mentoring?

Why do the trades have apprenticeships and professions require internships? Because personal attention from experienced practitioners helps learners master essential skills, techniques, attitudes, and knowledge.

In every culture throughout human history, mentoring has been the primary means of passing on knowledge and skills. The Bible is certainly filled with examples of mentoring: Eli and Samuel, Elijah and Elisha, Moses and Joshua, Naomi and Ruth, Elizabeth and Mary, Barnabas and Paul, Paul and Timothy. And, of course, Jesus and the disciples is a supreme example of mentoring.

Here's a pop quiz question:

A mentor is ...

    a) A model
    b) An encourager
    c) An imparter of knowledge
    d) All of the above

The answer is "d." A mentor may wear many different hats, but the one thing that all mentors share is the ability to listen and encourage. A mentor is a brain to pick, an ear to listen, and a push in the right direction.

We have helped coordinate thousands of marriage mentoring relationships over the years and we've come to a conclusion: there is no single way to be a marriage mentor; every mentoring relationship takes on its own personality. Yet the variance in these relationships still operates within certain parameters and that's what allows us to define our terms.

So here goes. We define a marriage mentor as *a relatively happy, more experienced couple purposefully investing in another couple to effectively navigate a journey that they have already taken.*

A marriage mentoring relationship can be short term or long term. It can be consistent and predictable or spontaneous and sporadic. While every marriage mentoring relationship has its own style that unfolds as the relationship develops, some potential confusion can be spared if the mentors and mentorees discuss their initial expectations of the relationship.

If you are interested in exploring the idea of becoming a marriage mentor, or finding a marriage mentor in your area, please visit our website at RealRelationships.com.

The Marriage
Mentoring Triad

Many churches find it helpful to consider marriage mentoring in three major areas or "tracks." It's what we call the Marriage Mentoring Triad:

MAXIMIZING
Deepening and enriching
stable marriages

PREPARING
Building solid
foundations
for engaged and
newlywed couples

REPAIRING
Encouraging
couples in
distress

How to Launch a Marriage Mentoring Ministry

- Read *The Complete Guide to Marriage Mentoring* by Les and Leslie Parrott.

- Become trained in the "10 Essential Skills of Marriage Mentoring" by using *The Complete Resource Kit for Marriage Mentoring* (including the his/her Training Manuals).

- Recruit and train three other mentor couples in your congregation so each one of them can coordinate one of the three tracks of the Marriage Mentoring Triad.

- Announce to the congregation that you are launching a marriage mentoring ministry and invite couples who would like to be mentored to sign up (the upcoming DVD by the Parrotts provides a video appropriate for playing to the congregation for this purpose).

- Go to RealRelationships.com and sign up for free mailings to help you maintain your marriage mentoring ministry.

- Pray that God would direct and bless the couples in your care who get involved in this lay-led ministry.

What's Your Excuse?

Both of us grew up in a parsonage. We've been involved in church work our entire lives. Les is an ordained minister. We also speak to hundreds of ministers annually. So we know you may have some reticence. You may be saying, "I don't need another program to administer." You're right. That's why marriage mentoring is low-maintenance. It belongs to the laity. Or maybe you're saying, "I can't get volunteers to teach classes, let alone mentor other couples." We understand. But recruiting mentor couples is easier than you think. Perhaps you're saying, "I don't want to detract from the marriage counseling program we've built up." It won't. In fact, it will augment it. "For now we're putting our energies into children's ministry and youth work." Worthy indeed. But marriage mentoring may be the most important thing you ever do for the young people in your church. Marriage mentoring can literally increase the spiritual vitality of your entire congregation.

The truth is, we can't think of a legitimate excuse for not having a marriage mentoring ministry in every local church, large or small. Why? Because couples of every age and stage can benefit from marriage mentoring, and it's easy for the local church to get going.

Not only that, but the Bible calls us to this kind of action. Marriage mentoring is a means by which you can fulfill Paul's injunction when he says the job of a pastor is "to prepare God's people for works of service" (Ephesians 4:12). What works of service could be of more value these days to the couples in your care than marriage mentoring?

The Complete Guide to Marriage Mentoring
Connecting Couples to Build Better Marriages

Drs. Les and Leslie Parrott

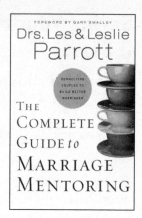

A comprehensive resource to help churches build a thriving marriage mentoring program.

Les and Leslie Parrott are passionate about how marriage mentoring can transform couples, families, and entire congregations. *The Complete Guide to Marriage Mentoring* includes life-changing insights and essential skills for

- Preparing engaged and newlywed couples
- Maximizing marriages from good to great
- Repairing marriages in distress

Practical guidelines help mentors and couples work together as a team, agree on outcomes, and develop skills for the marriage mentoring process. Appendixes offer a wealth of additional resources and tools. An exhaustive resource for marriage mentorship in any church setting, this guide also includes insights from interviews with church leaders and marriage mentors from around the country.

"The time is ripe for marriage mentoring, and this book is exactly what we need."

— Gary Smalley, author of *The DNA of Relationships*

Available in stores and online!

Saving Your Marriage Before It Starts

Seven Questions to Ask Before—and After—You Marry

Drs. Les and Leslie Parrott

Saving Your Marriage Before It Starts, created by relationship experts Drs. Les and Leslie Parrott, is a comprehensive marriage program designed specifically for today's couples by a couple. And now, in this updated edition, the Parrotts' award-winning approach has been expanded to incorporate ten more years of feedback, research, and professional experience.

This is more than a book—it's practically a self-guided premarital counseling course, and it is used by counselors and churches across the country and, now in ten languages, worldwide. Questions at the end of every chapter help you explore each topic personally. Companion men's and women's workbooks full of self-tests and exercises help you apply what you learn and enjoy intimate discussions along the way. There is even a seven-session DVD kit (with a bonus session for people entering a second marriage) available that you can use on your own or with other couples that want to grow together in a group or a class. In this dynamic DVD you'll not only hear entertaining and insightful teaching from the Parrotts, but you'll also meet other real-life couples who provide amazing candor and perspective.

Relationship experts Les and Leslie Parrott show you the secrets to building a marriage that lasts.

- Uncover the most important misbeliefs of marriage
- Learn how to communicate with instant understanding
- Discover the secret to reducing and resolving conflict
- Master the skills of money management
- Get your sex life off to a great start
- Understand the three essential ingredients to lasting love
- Discover the importance of becoming "soul mates" ... and more.

Make your marriage everything it is meant to be. Save your marriage—before (and after) it starts.

Love Talk

Speak Each Other's Language Like You Never Have Before

Drs. Les and Leslie Parrott

A breakthrough discovery in communication for transforming love relationships.

Over and over, couples consistently name "improved communication" as the greatest need in their relationships. *Love Talk*, by acclaimed relationship experts Drs. Les and Leslie Parrott, is a deep yet simple plan full of new insights that will revolutionize communication in love relationships.

In this no-nonsense book, "psychobabble" is translated into easy-to-understand language that clearly teaches you what you need to do — and not do — in order to speak each other's language like you never have before.

Love Talk includes:

- The Love Talk Indicator, a free personalized online assessment (a $30.00 value) to help you determine your unique talk style
- The Secret to Emotional Connection
- Charts and sample conversations
- The most important conversation you'll ever have
- A short course on Communication 101
- Appendix on Practical Help for the "Silent Partner"

Two softcover his and hers workbooks are full of lively exercises and enlightening self-tests that help couples apply what they are learning about communication directly to their relationships.

Available in stores and online!

Trading Places

The Secret to the Marriage You Want

Drs. Les and Leslie Parrott

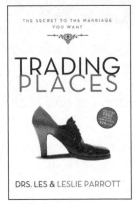

To understand your spouse you've got to walk in his or her shoes.

Ever feel like you're stepping on each other's toes? Then maybe it's time you put yourselves in each other's shoes. Of course that may sound uncomfortable. But it's easier than you think—and it will revolutionize your relationship. In fact, bestselling authors Drs. Les and Leslie Parrott reveal the little-known secrets of putting the time-tested strategy of trading places to work in your own marriage.

In this book, chock-full of practical helps and tips you've never thought of, you'll learn the three-step-strategy to trading places and, as a result, you're sure to:

- Increase your levels of passion
- Bolster your commitment
- Eliminate nagging
- Short-circuit conflict
- Double your laughter
- Forgive more quickly
- Talk more intimately

This book also features a powerful, free online assessment that instantly improves your inclination to trade places.

Most couples never discover the rewards of trading places. For example, did you know it's the quickest way to get your own needs met? It's true! And Les and Leslie show you how. They also disclose exactly how trading places improves your conversations and how it's guaranteed to fire up your sex life. Truly, your love life and your entire marriage will never be the same after you learn the intimate dance of trading places.

Available in stores and online!